TABLEAU

for Business Intelligence

Transforming Data into Actionable Insights

Kiet Huynh

Table of Contents

CHAPTER I
Introduction to Tableau and Power BI

1.1 Overview of Tableau

Tableau is a powerful and versatile data visualization and business intelligence tool that enables users to analyze and present data in an interactive and intuitive way. With its user-friendly interface and robust features, Tableau has become a preferred choice for data analysts, business professionals, and organizations seeking to derive insights from their data. In this section, we'll delve into an in-depth overview of Tableau, discussing its key features, components, and the advantages it offers for data analysis and visualization.

Key Features of Tableau:

Tableau boasts a rich set of features that make it a popular choice for data visualization and analysis:

1. Data Connectivity: Tableau can connect to a wide range of data sources, including databases, spreadsheets, cloud-based services, and web data connectors. Its ability to work with various data formats ensures that you can analyze data from different sources seamlessly.

2. Interactive Dashboards: Tableau allows users to create interactive and dynamic dashboards. You can build visualizations, charts, and maps, and then combine them into dashboards that provide a comprehensive view of your data. Users can interact with these dashboards to explore data further.

3. Drag-and-Drop Interface: One of Tableau's strengths is its ease of use. You can create visualizations by simply dragging and dropping data fields onto the canvas. This intuitive interface eliminates the need for complex coding, making it accessible to a broad audience.

4. Data Blending and Joining: Tableau supports data blending, enabling you to combine data from multiple sources. You can also perform data joins, unions, and cross-database joins to integrate and analyze data effectively.

5. Custom Calculations: Tableau provides a rich set of functions for creating custom calculations. Whether you need to perform statistical analysis, create calculated fields, or define parameters, Tableau offers flexibility for advanced data manipulation.

6. Mapping and Geospatial Analysis: With Tableau, you can visualize geographic data and perform geospatial analysis. It supports various map types, allowing you to create heat maps, custom territories, and more.

7. Collaboration and Sharing: Tableau enables users to publish their visualizations and dashboards on Tableau Server or Tableau Online, making it easy to share insights within your organization. Permissions, security, and governance features provide control over who can access and edit your content.

8. Scalability: Tableau is scalable and can accommodate both small and large datasets. It can handle real-time data streaming, making it suitable for organizations with diverse data needs.

Examples:

Let's consider an example to illustrate how Tableau can be used in practice. Imagine you work for a retail company and want to analyze sales data. Using Tableau, you can:

1. Connect to your sales database or import data from Excel.

2. Create a bar chart to visualize the sales performance of different product categories.

3. Add a filter that allows you to select a specific time period.

4. Build a dashboard that combines this bar chart with a map showing the geographical distribution of sales.

5. Publish this dashboard on Tableau Server for your team to access and interact with.

Steps:

1. Open Tableau Desktop.

2. Connect to your data source.

3. Drag the "Product Category" field to the Columns shelf.

4. Drag the "Sales" field to the Rows shelf.

5. Create a filter by dragging the "Date" field to the Filters shelf.

6. Build a map by dragging the "Location" field to the Marks card.

7. Save the workbook and publish it to Tableau Server.

By following these steps, you can create an interactive sales analysis dashboard that allows users to explore data and gain insights.

In conclusion, Tableau is a versatile tool that empowers users to transform data into actionable insights through interactive visualizations and dashboards. Its user-friendly interface and extensive capabilities make it an invaluable asset for data professionals and businesses seeking to harness the power of their data. In the upcoming sections of this book, we will explore Tableau's features in greater detail, ensuring that you can harness its full potential.

1.2 Overview of Power BI

Power BI is a robust and widely-used business intelligence and data visualization tool developed by Microsoft. It empowers users to transform raw data into meaningful insights and visually appealing reports and dashboards. In this section, we will provide a comprehensive overview of Power BI, including its key features, components, and how to get started with using it effectively.

Key Features of Power BI:

Power BI offers a variety of features that make it a popular choice for data analysis and visualization:

1. Data Connectivity: Power BI supports extensive data source connectivity, allowing you to connect to databases, cloud services, and web-based data. You can import, transform, and model your data to make it suitable for analysis.

2. Drag-and-Drop Interface: Much like Tableau, Power BI provides a user-friendly interface that requires no coding. You can simply drag and drop fields onto the canvas to create visualizations, reports, and dashboards.

3. Data Modeling and Transformation: Power BI provides a powerful data modeling engine that allows you to create relationships between tables, define measures, and perform data transformations. This feature is essential for working with complex datasets.

4. Custom Visualizations: While Power BI comes with a rich library of built-in visualizations, you can also extend its capabilities by importing custom visualizations from the Power BI marketplace. This flexibility allows you to create unique and tailored reports.

5. DAX (Data Analysis Expressions): DAX is a formula language used in Power BI for creating custom calculations and aggregations. With DAX, you can perform advanced calculations and create calculated columns and tables.

6. Power Query: Power Query is a data transformation tool integrated into Power BI. It allows you to connect to various data sources, clean and shape data, and create reusable queries for data preparation.

7. Power BI Service: Power BI offers a cloud-based service that allows you to publish and share reports and dashboards with stakeholders. You can also collaborate with others in real-time, making it a great tool for team-based projects.

8. Integration with Microsoft Products: Power BI seamlessly integrates with other Microsoft products like Excel, SharePoint, and Azure. This interoperability provides additional resources and capabilities for data analysis and sharing.

Examples:

Let's consider an example to illustrate how Power BI can be used in a real-world scenario. Imagine you work for a sales department in a retail company and need to analyze monthly sales performance. Here's how you can use Power BI:

1. Import your sales data into Power BI using Power Query.

2. Create a data model by defining relationships between the "Sales," "Products," and "Customers" tables.

3. Build a report with visualizations like bar charts, line charts, and tables to display sales trends and customer demographics.

4. Create a dashboard that combines these visualizations, making it easy to monitor sales performance.

Steps:

1. Open Power BI Desktop.

2. Click on "Get Data" to import your sales data from an Excel spreadsheet or a database.

3. Use the Power Query Editor to transform and shape your data.

4. Create relationships between tables in the "Model" view.

5. Design visualizations by dragging fields onto the report canvas.

6. Build a dashboard by pinning visualizations to it.

7. Publish your report to the Power BI Service for sharing with colleagues.

By following these steps, you can use Power BI to analyze and visualize your sales data effectively.

In conclusion, Power BI is a versatile business intelligence tool that provides users with a powerful platform for transforming data into actionable insights. Its user-friendly interface, data modeling capabilities, and cloud-based sharing options make it a top choice for data professionals and organizations. In the following chapters, we will delve deeper into Power BI's features and functionalities, ensuring you can harness its full potential for data analysis and visualization.

1.3 Key capabilities and benefits of Tableau

Tableau is a leading data visualization and business intelligence tool that offers a wide range of capabilities and benefits for data analysis. In this section, we will explore the key capabilities and advantages of Tableau, with specific examples and step-by-step guidance on how to leverage these capabilities effectively.

Key Capabilities of Tableau:

1. Data Connectivity: Tableau's ability to connect to various data sources is a fundamental strength. It can connect to databases, spreadsheets, web data connectors, and cloud-based platforms. Here's how you can leverage this capability:

   - Example: Connect to a SQL database by providing connection details, and start analyzing data directly from the source.

2. Interactive Visualizations: Tableau allows users to create interactive and visually appealing charts, graphs, and maps. You can build various types of visualizations and customize them to meet your specific needs. Here's how:

   - Example: Create a bar chart to display sales data, and enable interactivity by allowing users to filter data by category or time period.

3. Data Blending and Joining: Tableau supports data blending, enabling you to combine data from multiple sources, and perform joins and unions. This is particularly useful for integrating data from different departments or systems. Here's how:

   - Example: Blend data from your sales database with data from your marketing database to gain insights into how marketing campaigns impact sales.

4. Custom Calculations: With Tableau, you can create custom calculations and define calculated fields using a formula language. This is helpful for performing advanced data manipulation and analysis. Here's how:

   - Example: Calculate the profit margin by creating a custom calculated field that subtracts the cost from the revenue and divides by the revenue.

5. Mapping and Geospatial Analysis: Tableau provides robust mapping capabilities, allowing you to visualize geographic data and perform geospatial analysis. You can plot locations on maps and create custom territories. Here's how:

   - Example: Use longitude and latitude data to plot customer locations on a map, allowing you to identify regions with the highest customer concentration.

6. Dashboard Creation: Tableau enables users to create interactive dashboards that combine multiple visualizations. Dashboards provide a comprehensive view of data and facilitate storytelling. Here's how:

   - Example: Build a sales performance dashboard that displays sales trends, a geographical sales map, and key performance indicators (KPIs) in one view.

Benefits of Using Tableau:

1. Data-Driven Decision-Making: Tableau empowers organizations to make data-driven decisions by providing easy access to data and the tools to analyze it effectively. This results in better business outcomes.

2. User-Friendly Interface: Tableau's intuitive, drag-and-drop interface makes it accessible to users with varying levels of technical expertise. You don't need to be a programmer to create compelling visualizations.

3. Real-Time Data Analysis: Tableau can handle real-time data streams, allowing users to analyze live data and respond to changes promptly. This is valuable for monitoring and making quick decisions.

4. Sharing and Collaboration: Tableau offers options for sharing insights and collaborating with team members. You can publish dashboards to Tableau Server or Tableau Online, ensuring that stakeholders have access to the latest data.

5. Scalability: Whether you're working with small or large datasets, Tableau is scalable. It can adapt to the needs of your organization, making it suitable for businesses of all sizes.

Steps to Leverage Tableau's Capabilities:

Let's take an example to demonstrate how to leverage Tableau's capabilities. Suppose you want to create a dashboard to analyze the sales performance of different product categories. Here are the steps:

1. Connect to Data: Open Tableau and connect to your sales database.

2. Create Visualizations: Build bar charts for each product category to show sales trends.

3. Interactive Filters: Add filters for the date range and product category, allowing users to interact with the data.

4. Dashboard: Combine these charts into a dashboard and arrange them to provide a comprehensive view.

5. Publish: Publish the dashboard to Tableau Server for sharing with your team.

By following these steps, you can effectively leverage Tableau's capabilities to create an insightful sales performance dashboard.

In conclusion, Tableau offers a wide array of capabilities and benefits that make it a powerful tool for data analysis and visualization. Its user-friendly interface, data connectivity options, and interactive features enable users to transform data into actionable insights. Throughout this book, we will explore these capabilities in detail, equipping you with the skills to become a proficient data analyst and storyteller using Tableau.

1.4 Key capabilities and benefits of Power BI

Power BI, developed by Microsoft, is a robust and widely-used business intelligence tool that offers a range of capabilities and benefits for data analysis and visualization. In this section, we will delve into the key capabilities and advantages of Power BI, providing specific examples and step-by-step guidance on how to make the most of these capabilities.

Key Capabilities of Power BI:

1. Data Connectivity: Power BI is renowned for its ability to connect to various data sources. It supports connections to databases, cloud services, web data connectors, and more. Here's how you can leverage this capability:

  - Example: Connect Power BI to a SQL Server database and import data directly from the database tables.

2. Drag-and-Drop Interface: Much like Tableau, Power BI offers a user-friendly drag-and-drop interface. You can easily create visualizations and reports without the need for extensive coding or technical skills. Here's how:

  - Example: Drag and drop fields onto the canvas to create a bar chart that displays sales data by product category.

3. Data Modeling and Transformation: Power BI provides robust data modeling and transformation capabilities. Users can define relationships between tables, create calculated columns, and perform data transformations. Here's how:

  - Example: Define a relationship between a "Sales" table and a "Products" table to analyze how products contribute to sales.

4. Custom Visualizations: Power BI includes a wide range of built-in visualizations, and users can extend this library with custom visuals from the Power BI marketplace. This flexibility allows for the creation of tailored and unique reports. Here's how:

   - Example: Import a custom visual from the Power BI marketplace to create a unique visualization that effectively conveys your data.

5. DAX (Data Analysis Expressions): Power BI uses DAX, a formula language, for creating custom calculations and aggregations. DAX provides advanced calculations and insights. Here's how:

   - Example: Create a DAX formula to calculate the year-over-year growth in sales for a specific product.

6. Power Query: Integrated into Power BI, Power Query allows users to connect to various data sources, clean and shape data, and create reusable queries for data preparation. Here's how:

   - Example: Use Power Query to connect to a web data source, extract specific data, and transform it into a suitable format for analysis.

7. Power BI Service: Power BI offers a cloud-based service that allows you to publish and share reports and dashboards. It enables real-time collaboration and sharing with team members and stakeholders. Here's how:

   - Example: Publish a Power BI report to the Power BI Service, where your team can access it, view real-time data, and make comments for collaboration.

8. Integration with Microsoft Products: Power BI seamlessly integrates with other Microsoft products such as Excel, SharePoint, and Azure, providing additional resources and capabilities for data analysis and sharing. Here's how:

   - Example: Embed a Power BI report into a SharePoint site to make it accessible to a broader audience within your organization.

Benefits of Using Power BI:

1. Data-Driven Decision-Making: Power BI empowers organizations to make data-driven decisions by providing easy access to data and tools for analysis. This results in improved business outcomes.

2. User-Friendly Interface: Power BI's intuitive drag-and-drop interface makes it accessible to users with various levels of technical expertise. You can quickly create compelling visualizations and reports.

3. Real-Time Data Analysis: Power BI can handle real-time data streams, enabling users to analyze live data and respond to changes promptly. This is valuable for monitoring and making quick decisions.

4. Sharing and Collaboration: Power BI offers options for sharing insights and collaborating with team members. You can publish dashboards to the Power BI Service, ensuring that stakeholders have access to the latest data.

5. Scalability: Whether you're working with small or large datasets, Power BI is scalable. It can adapt to the needs of your organization, making it suitable for businesses of all sizes.

Steps to Leverage Power BI's Capabilities:

Let's illustrate how to leverage Power BI's capabilities with an example. Suppose you want to create a dashboard to analyze the sales performance of different product categories. Here are the steps:

1. Connect to Data: Open Power BI Desktop and connect to your sales database.

2. Create Visualizations: Build visualizations such as bar charts, pie charts, and tables to represent sales data.

3. Data Modeling: Define relationships between tables and create measures for calculations.

4. Dashboard Creation: Combine the visualizations into a dashboard to provide an overview of sales performance.

5. Publish and Share: Publish the dashboard to the Power BI Service, where your team can access it, collaborate, and explore real-time data.

By following these steps, you can effectively leverage Power BI's capabilities to create insightful sales performance dashboards.

In conclusion, Power BI offers a wide array of capabilities and benefits, making it a powerful tool for data analysis and visualization. Its user-friendly interface, data connectivity options, and cloud-based sharing features empower users to transform data into actionable insights. In the upcoming chapters, we will explore these capabilities in detail, equipping you with the skills to become a proficient data analyst and storyteller using Power BI.

1.5 When to use Tableau

Tableau is a versatile data visualization and business intelligence tool that can be used in a variety of situations. Understanding when to use Tableau is crucial for making the most of its capabilities. In this section, we'll explore specific scenarios and provide examples of when Tableau is the ideal choice. We'll also guide you through the process of determining when to use Tableau effectively.

When to Use Tableau:

1. Exploratory Data Analysis (EDA):

- *Scenario:* You have a large dataset with various dimensions and measures, and you want to explore the data to identify patterns, trends, and anomalies.

- *Example:* You have sales data for multiple products, regions, and time periods. You use Tableau to quickly visualize and interact with the data, identifying which products perform best in different regions over time.

- *Steps:*

  - Import your dataset into Tableau.

  - Create visualizations like scatter plots, bar charts, and heat maps to explore relationships within the data.

  - Use filters and parameters to narrow down the analysis.

2. Data Storytelling:

- *Scenario:* You need to communicate your data findings effectively to stakeholders, and you want to create engaging data narratives.

- *Example:* You want to present your company's quarterly sales performance to the management team. Tableau helps you build interactive dashboards that tell a compelling story, showing trends and explaining the factors driving sales.

- *Steps:*

  - Create a dashboard with a sequence of visualizations that convey the story.

  - Use annotations and tooltips to provide context and explanations.

3. Real-Time Data Monitoring:

- *Scenario:* You have data streams or databases that are updated in real-time, and you need to monitor key metrics and trends as they occur.

- *Example:* You work in a call center, and you want to monitor incoming call volume, customer wait times, and service agent performance in real-time. Tableau's live data connections help you achieve this.

- *Steps:*

  - Connect Tableau to your real-time data source.

  - Set up dashboards to update automatically at short intervals, such as every few seconds.

4. Geospatial Analysis:

- *Scenario:* Your data includes location-based information, and you want to visualize and analyze it on maps.

- *Example:* You work for a delivery company and need to optimize delivery routes. Tableau's mapping capabilities enable you to plot customer locations, traffic data, and delivery routes.

- *Steps:*

  - Import data with latitude and longitude coordinates.

  - Use maps to visualize data points and geospatial relationships.

5. Custom Calculations and Advanced Analytics:

- *Scenario:* You need to perform complex calculations and advanced analytics on your data.

- *Example:* You are a financial analyst and want to create financial models, perform regression analysis, or calculate risk metrics. Tableau's integration with R and Python allows you to perform advanced calculations.

- *Steps:*

  - Use calculated fields and custom calculations.

  - Leverage integration with R or Python for advanced analytics.

6. Publishing and Sharing Insights:

- *Scenario:* You want to share data insights and dashboards with colleagues and stakeholders in a secure and controlled manner.

- *Example:* You've created a quarterly sales report, and you want your sales team to access it from different locations. Tableau Server or Tableau Online allows you to publish and share securely.

  - *Steps:*

    - Publish your workbook to Tableau Server or Tableau Online.

    - Configure permissions and access controls.

Determining When to Use Tableau:

When deciding whether to use Tableau, consider the following steps:

1. Assess Data Complexity: Examine the complexity of your data. If you have extensive data with multiple dimensions, Tableau's capabilities for data exploration and visualization are valuable.

2. Consider the Audience: Think about who will use the data and reports. If the audience includes non-technical users, Tableau's user-friendly interface is advantageous.

3. Real-Time or Periodic Analysis: Determine whether you need real-time data analysis or periodic reporting. Tableau's live data connections are suitable for real-time analysis.

4. Data Sources: Check the compatibility of your data sources with Tableau. Ensure that you can easily connect to your data.

5. Custom Calculations and Analytics: If you require advanced calculations or custom analytics, Tableau's capabilities for creating calculated fields and integrating with R and Python are beneficial.

6. Sharing and Collaboration: If you need to share insights within your organization and collaborate with others, Tableau Server or Tableau Online provides secure sharing options.

By following these steps and considering your specific needs, you can determine when to use Tableau effectively, making it a valuable tool for your data analysis and visualization projects.

In conclusion, Tableau is a versatile tool that can be used in various scenarios to explore data, tell data-driven stories, monitor real-time data, analyze geospatial information, perform advanced analytics, and share insights securely. Understanding when and how to use Tableau is key to maximizing its potential in your data-related projects.

1.6 When to use Power BI

Power BI is a versatile business intelligence tool that can be employed in various scenarios to analyze data and create compelling reports and dashboards. In this section, we'll explore specific situations and provide examples of when Power BI is the ideal choice. We'll also guide you through the process of determining when to use Power BI effectively.

When to Use Power BI:

1. Data Exploration and Analysis:

- *Scenario:* You have a dataset with complex data structures, and you want to explore and analyze it effectively.

- *Example:* You work for an e-commerce company and need to analyze customer behavior data, including clickstreams and purchase histories. Power BI enables you to create insightful visualizations and conduct in-depth data analysis.

- *Steps:*

  - Connect Power BI to your data source.

  - Use Power Query to clean and transform data.

  - Create visualizations such as line charts, histograms, and tables for in-depth data exploration.

2. Data Reporting and Dashboarding:

- *Scenario:* You want to create interactive and visually appealing reports and dashboards to communicate data insights to your team or stakeholders.

- *Example:* You are a project manager and need to provide project status updates to your team and stakeholders. Power BI allows you to build dashboards that show project progress, budgets, and timelines.

- *Steps:*

  - Import data into Power BI.

  - Design a dashboard with various visualizations, filters, and slicers.

  - Share the dashboard with your team using Power BI Service.

3. Real-Time Data Monitoring:

- *Scenario:* You have data sources that update in real-time, and you need to monitor key metrics and trends as they occur.

- *Example:* You work in a call center and want to monitor incoming call volume, customer wait times, and service agent performance in real-time. Power BI's real-time dashboards help you achieve this.

- *Steps:*

  - Connect Power BI to your real-time data source.

  - Create a dashboard that updates at regular intervals, such as every few seconds, to reflect real-time changes.

4. Geospatial and Location Analysis:

- *Scenario:* Your data contains location-based information, and you want to visualize and analyze it using maps.

- *Example:* You are in the retail industry and need to analyze the distribution of your stores and their performance. Power BI's mapping capabilities allow you to plot store locations, visualize sales data, and analyze performance by region.

- *Steps:*

  - Import data with geographic coordinates.

  - Utilize Power BI's map visuals to display location-based data.

5. Advanced Calculations and Data Modeling:

- *Scenario:* You need to perform complex calculations, create calculated measures, or build data models for forecasting and predictions.

- *Example:* You work in finance and need to create financial models, calculate financial ratios, and perform predictive analysis. Power BI's DAX (Data Analysis Expressions) language is a powerful tool for these tasks.

- *Steps:*

  - Use DAX to create calculated columns and measures.

  - Build data models that enable predictive analysis and data forecasting.

6. Sharing and Collaboration:

- *Scenario:* You want to share data insights and reports with colleagues and stakeholders in a secure and controlled manner.

- *Example:* You've created a quarterly sales report, and you want your sales team to access it from different locations. Power BI Service allows you to publish, share, and collaborate securely.

- *Steps:*

  - Publish your Power BI report to the Power BI Service.

  - Configure access permissions and share the report with authorized users.

Determining When to Use Power BI:

To determine when to use Power BI, follow these steps:

1. Analyze Data Complexity: Assess the complexity of your data. If it contains multiple dimensions and complex relationships, Power BI's capabilities for data modeling and visualization are beneficial.

2. Consider the Audience: Think about who will use the reports and dashboards. If the audience includes both technical and non-technical users, Power BI's user-friendly interface is advantageous.

3. Real-Time or Periodic Analysis: Determine whether you require real-time data analysis or periodic reporting. Power BI's real-time dashboards are suitable for monitoring changing data.

4. Data Sources: Verify that your data sources are compatible with Power BI. Ensure that you can connect to your data efficiently.

5. Custom Calculations and Analytics: If you need to perform advanced calculations, create measures, and build data models for forecasting, Power BI's DAX language is a valuable resource.

6. Sharing and Collaboration: If you need to share insights within your organization and collaborate with others, Power BI Service offers secure sharing options.

By considering these steps and your specific needs, you can determine when to use Power BI effectively, making it a valuable tool for your data analysis and reporting projects.

In conclusion, Power BI is a versatile tool suitable for data exploration, reporting, real-time monitoring, geospatial analysis, advanced calculations, and secure sharing of insights. Understanding when and how to use Power BI is key to maximizing its potential in your data-related projects.

1.7 Comparing Tableau and Power BI

Tableau and Power BI are two popular tools for data analysis and visualization, and understanding the differences and similarities between them can help you make an informed decision when choosing the right tool for your specific needs. In this section, we will compare Tableau and Power BI in terms of key aspects, providing specific examples and step-by-step guidance for making comparisons.

1. Data Connectivity:

- **Tableau:** Tableau offers a wide range of data connectivity options. You can connect to databases, spreadsheets, cloud services, web data connectors, and more. The process of connecting to data sources is straightforward, and it supports real-time data connectivity.

- **Power BI:** Power BI also supports various data sources, including databases, cloud services, and web data connectors. It offers native integration with Microsoft services such as Azure and Excel. Connecting to data is user-friendly and efficient.

Comparison: Both Tableau and Power BI provide robust data connectivity options. The choice between them may depend on your specific data sources and integration needs.

2. User Interface:

- **Tableau:** Tableau's user interface is known for its drag-and-drop simplicity. It provides a canvas where you can create visualizations and dashboards by dragging fields onto the workspace. Users with varying technical backgrounds can quickly get started.

- **Power BI:** Power BI also offers an intuitive, user-friendly interface. You can create reports and dashboards by dragging and dropping fields onto the canvas. It is particularly suited for users who are familiar with other Microsoft products.

Comparison: Both Tableau and Power BI provide user-friendly interfaces with similar drag-and-drop functionality. The choice may depend on your team's familiarity with Microsoft products.

3. Data Visualization:

- **Tableau:** Tableau offers a wide variety of built-in visualization options, including bar charts, scatter plots, maps, and more. Customization options are extensive, allowing for in-depth visual design.

- **Power BI:** Power BI provides a broad selection of built-in visuals and allows users to extend the library with custom visuals from the marketplace. It offers extensive customization options for visual elements.

Comparison: Both Tableau and Power BI excel in data visualization, offering a variety of options and customization features.

4. Advanced Analytics:

- **Tableau:** Tableau provides advanced analytics capabilities through integration with R and Python. Users can create calculated fields and perform statistical analysis using built-in functions.

- **Power BI:** Power BI offers advanced analytics through DAX (Data Analysis Expressions), a formula language similar to Excel. It allows users to create calculated measures, columns, and perform complex calculations.

Comparison: Tableau's integration with R and Python may be preferred for advanced statistical analysis, while Power BI's DAX language is powerful for creating complex calculations.

5. Real-Time Data:

- **Tableau:** Tableau can handle real-time data sources and provide real-time monitoring through its live data connections. Users can set up automatic data refresh intervals for real-time dashboards.

- **Power BI:** Power BI also supports real-time data, allowing users to connect to real-time data sources and create live dashboards that update at regular intervals.

Comparison: Both Tableau and Power BI offer real-time data capabilities, making them suitable for monitoring and reacting to live data.

6. Collaboration and Sharing:

- **Tableau:** Tableau provides options for sharing insights and dashboards through Tableau Server and Tableau Online. Users can collaborate and comment on reports, and it offers fine-grained access control.

- **Power BI:** Power BI offers sharing and collaboration through the Power BI Service. Users can publish reports, share them with colleagues, and collaborate in real-time. It integrates seamlessly with other Microsoft services like SharePoint.

Comparison: Both Tableau and Power BI offer robust sharing and collaboration options. The choice may depend on your organization's existing technology stack.

7. Cost:

- **Tableau:** Tableau's pricing model includes both individual and enterprise-level licensing. It can be considered more expensive, especially for smaller organizations.

- **Power BI:** Power BI offers a free version (Power BI Desktop) and a paid version (Power BI Pro). The paid version is cost-effective for small to medium-sized organizations.

Comparison: Power BI is often considered more cost-effective, especially for smaller businesses, due to its free version and competitive pricing.

8. Ecosystem and Integration:

- **Tableau:** Tableau has a strong ecosystem with a marketplace for extensions, connectors, and custom visuals. It integrates with a variety of third-party tools and services.

- **Power BI:** Power BI leverages the Microsoft ecosystem and offers seamless integration with Azure, Excel, SharePoint, and other Microsoft services. It also has a marketplace for custom visuals and extensions.

Comparison: The choice between Tableau and Power BI may depend on your existing technology ecosystem and the specific tools and services you need to integrate.

Determining Which Tool to Use:

To determine whether to use Tableau or Power BI, consider the following factors:

1. Data Sources: Analyze your data sources and their compatibility with both tools.

2. User Familiarity: Consider the familiarity of your team with either Tableau or Microsoft products.

3. Advanced Analytics: Assess your need for advanced analytics and the language or tools required for your analysis.

4. Cost: Evaluate your budget and the licensing options that best suit your organization.

5. Ecosystem and Integration: Consider your existing technology stack and the tools or services you need to integrate with.

In conclusion, both Tableau and Power BI are powerful tools for data analysis and visualization, and the choice between them depends on various factors, including data sources, user familiarity, analytical requirements, cost, and integration needs. Understanding the differences and similarities between these tools is essential for making an informed decision in your specific context.

CHAPTER II
Getting Started with Tableau

2.1 Installing and setting up Tableau

Tableau is a powerful data analysis and visualization tool that offers both desktop and online versions. In this section, we will guide you through the process of installing Tableau Desktop and setting it up on your computer. We'll provide step-by-step instructions and specific examples to help you get started with Tableau.

Step 1: Download Tableau Desktop:

1. Visit the official Tableau website at https://www.tableau.com.

2. Navigate to the "Products" section, and click on "Tableau Desktop."

3. You'll be prompted to sign in or create a Tableau account. If you're a new user, you can create an account by providing your details.

4. After signing in or creating an account, you'll be directed to the Tableau Desktop download page. Select the appropriate version for your operating system (Windows or macOS).

5. Click the "Download" button to start downloading the Tableau Desktop installer.

Step 2: Install Tableau Desktop:

Once the installer is downloaded, follow these steps to install Tableau Desktop on your computer:

For Windows:

1. Locate the downloaded installer (typically in your "Downloads" folder) and double-click on it.

2. The Tableau Desktop installation wizard will open. Click "Next" to begin the installation.

3. Review the license agreement and accept the terms if you agree.

4. Choose the installation directory and click "Next."

5. Select whether you want a desktop shortcut and a start menu folder, then click "Next."

6. Review the installation settings and click "Install."

7. Wait for the installation process to complete.

8. Click "Finish" to exit the installation wizard.

For macOS:

1. Locate the downloaded installer, which is usually in your "Downloads" folder, and double-click on it.

2. A new window will appear with the Tableau Desktop application. Drag the Tableau icon into the "Applications" folder to install it.

3. Wait for the copying process to finish.

4. Once the Tableau Desktop application is in your "Applications" folder, you can open it from there.

Step 3: Activate Tableau Desktop:

After installing Tableau Desktop, you'll need to activate it. Here's how:

1. Open Tableau Desktop by clicking on its icon or searching for it in your applications.

2. When Tableau Desktop opens, you will be prompted to activate it. Enter your Tableau account credentials (the same ones you used to download Tableau).

3. After entering your credentials, Tableau will verify your account, and the software will be activated for use.

Step 4: Tableau Interface and Setup:

Once Tableau Desktop is installed and activated, you can start using it. Here's a brief overview of the Tableau interface and setup:

- **Workspace:** The main workspace is divided into several sections, including the data pane, the connection pane, and the canvas. Familiarize yourself with these areas, as you'll be using them to work with data.

- **Data Connection:** To connect to your data source, click on "Connect to Data" in the data pane. You can connect to various data sources, such as databases, spreadsheets, and cloud services.

- **Data Source Setup:** Once you've connected to your data source, you can set up your data source by specifying tables and fields to use in your analysis.

- **Visualizations:** Create visualizations by dragging and dropping fields onto the canvas. You can choose from various chart types, including bar charts, line charts, and scatter plots.

- **Toolbar:** The toolbar at the top of the Tableau interface provides access to various tools and options for designing and formatting your visualizations.

Example: Getting Started with Tableau

Let's say you want to create a bar chart that displays the sales data of your company. Here's how you can get started:

1. Open Tableau Desktop.

2. Click "Connect to Data" in the data pane.

3. Choose your data source (e.g., an Excel spreadsheet) and connect to it.

4. In the data source setup, select the sales data table and the relevant fields (e.g., date and sales amount).

5. Drag the "Date" field to the columns shelf and the "Sales Amount" field to the rows shelf.

6. Tableau will automatically generate a bar chart displaying your sales data.

7. Use the toolbar to format and customize the chart as needed.

By following these steps, you can quickly create your first visualization in Tableau.

In conclusion, installing and setting up Tableau Desktop is a straightforward process that involves downloading, installing, and activating the software. Once you're set up, you can start using Tableau's intuitive interface to connect to data sources, create visualizations, and begin your data analysis journey.

2.2 Interface and navigation

Tableau provides a user-friendly and intuitive interface that empowers users to create data visualizations and perform data analysis efficiently. In this section, we'll explore the key elements of the Tableau interface and provide step-by-step instructions for navigating through it. We'll also use specific examples to illustrate how to work with Tableau effectively.

Tableau Interface Overview:

The Tableau interface consists of various components, each serving a specific purpose. Let's take a closer look at the key elements:

1. Menu Bar: The menu bar at the top provides access to essential functions like file management, data connection, and formatting.

2. Toolbar: The toolbar, located just below the menu bar, offers quick access to commonly used tools and actions, including data source connection, undo/redo, and visualization formatting.

3. Data Pane: On the left side of the interface, the data pane displays a hierarchical view of your data source, including tables, fields, and data source options. This is where you manage your data connections.

4. Connections Pane: Below the data pane, the connections pane shows your current data source connection and provides options for data source management.

5. Canvas: The central workspace is your canvas, where you create and design visualizations. You'll drag and drop fields onto the canvas to build your charts and dashboards.

6. Shelves: Located above the canvas, the shelves include rows, columns, pages, and marks cards. These shelves are where you place fields to define the structure and content of your visualizations.

7. Sheets and Dashboards: On the lower part of the interface, you'll find tabs for sheets (individual visualizations) and dashboards (collections of multiple sheets). You can switch between sheets and dashboards here.

Navigating the Tableau Interface:

Now that you're familiar with the key elements of the Tableau interface, let's go through the process of navigating and working within Tableau:

Step 1: Connecting to Data:

1. Click on the "Connect to Data" button in the data pane to begin your analysis. Select the data source type (e.g., Excel, database, web data connector) and connect to your data.

2. In the data source setup, select the appropriate tables and fields to use in your analysis.

Step 2: Building Visualizations:

1. To create a visualization, drag a field from the data pane to the rows shelf to define the rows of your chart. For example, dragging "Product Category" might create a bar chart with each category as a row.

2. Drag another field to the columns shelf to define the columns of your chart, such as "Sales Amount."

3. Tableau will generate a default visualization based on your selections.

4. Use the marks card to adjust the level of detail, color, and size of the marks in your visualization.

5. You can also use filters, parameters, and calculated fields to refine your visualization further.

Step 3: Formatting and Styling:

1. Use the toolbar to format and style your visualization. You can adjust colors, fonts, borders, and labels to make your visualization more appealing and informative.

2. Apply sorting and grouping to your data to organize it logically.

3. Use the dashboard tab to create a dashboard and combine multiple visualizations into one cohesive view.

Step 4: Saving and Sharing:

1. Save your workbook by clicking "File" in the menu bar and selecting "Save" or "Save As." This allows you to revisit and edit your work later.

2. Share your work with others by publishing it to Tableau Server, Tableau Online, or exporting it as an image or PDF.

Example: Creating a Simple Bar Chart in Tableau:

Let's say you have a dataset of product sales, and you want to create a simple bar chart showing sales by product category. Here's how to do it:

1. Connect to your data source by clicking "Connect to Data" and selecting your dataset.

2. Drag the "Product Category" field to the rows shelf and the "Sales Amount" field to the columns shelf.

3. Tableau will automatically generate a bar chart showing sales by product category.

4. You can further customize your chart by adjusting colors, labels, and formatting using the toolbar and formatting options.

By following these steps, you can create your first visualization in Tableau.

In conclusion, Tableau's interface is designed to be user-friendly and efficient, allowing users to navigate through the data connection, visualization creation, formatting, and sharing processes seamlessly. Understanding the key elements of the interface and how to work with them is crucial for effective data analysis and visualization in Tableau.

2.3 Connecting to data sources

Tableau's power lies in its ability to connect to various data sources, allowing you to transform raw data into insightful visualizations. In this section, we'll dive into the process of connecting to data sources in Tableau, providing detailed guidance and practical examples.

Step 1: Launch Tableau:

1. Open Tableau Desktop on your computer.

Step 2: Connect to Data:

1. Upon launching Tableau, you'll be presented with the "Start Page." Click on "Connect to Data" to initiate the data connection process.

2. A new window will open with various data source options, including:

 - **File:** Connect to local files such as Excel, CSV, and text files.

 - **Server:** Connect to data stored on databases, cloud services, and other servers.

 - **Web Data Connector:** Extract data from web-based APIs and data sources.

 - **Data Server:** Connect to data sources published on Tableau Server or Tableau Online.

3. Select the appropriate data source option based on your data location and type.

Step 3: Connecting to Different Data Sources:

A. Connecting to Local Files (e.g., Excel):

1. Select "File" and choose the file type (e.g., Excel).

2. Browse and locate the file on your computer.

3. Click on the file to connect.

4. Tableau will display a preview of the data in the file. You can click on the sheet name to select a specific table.

5. Click "Connect" to load the data into Tableau.

B. Connecting to Databases (e.g., SQL Server):

1. Select "Server" and choose your database type (e.g., Microsoft SQL Server).

2. Enter the server details, including the server name, database name, and authentication method.

3. Provide your login credentials (username and password).

4. Click "Sign In" or "Connect" to establish the connection.

5. After connecting, you'll see a list of tables or views in your database. Select the ones you want to work with and click "Add."

C. Using Web Data Connectors (e.g., JSON API):

1. Select "Web Data Connector."

2. Enter the URL of the web data connector that provides the data you want to use.

3. Click "Connect" to initiate the connection.

4. You may be prompted to enter additional parameters or API keys, depending on the web data connector.

D. Connecting to Data Servers (e.g., Tableau Server):

1. Select "Data Server" and enter the server details, including the server name or URL.

2. Log in using your Tableau Server credentials.

3. After connecting, you can access data sources published on the server and select the one you want to work with.

Step 4: Data Source Setup:

1. After connecting to your data source, Tableau will display a preview of your data. You can see the data tables and fields.

2. Use the data source setup area to refine your data connection. You can rename tables, specify custom SQL queries, and add calculated fields.

3. To modify data source settings, click on the "Data Source" tab at the bottom of the screen.

4. You can join multiple tables, create relationships, and perform data blending to prepare your data for analysis.

Example: Connecting to an Excel File:

Let's assume you have an Excel file named "SalesData.xlsx" that contains sales data, and you want to connect to it in Tableau.

1. Launch Tableau Desktop.

2. Click "Connect to Data" from the Start Page.

3. Select "File" and then "Excel."

4. Browse and locate the "SalesData.xlsx" file on your computer.

5. Click on the file, and Tableau will display a preview of the data in the file.

6. Click "Connect" to load the data into Tableau.

7. Now, you can start building visualizations and performing data analysis on your sales data.

In conclusion, connecting to data sources in Tableau is a crucial first step in your data analysis journey. Tableau offers various options for connecting to local files, databases, web data sources, and data servers. By following the steps and examples outlined in this section, you can efficiently connect to your data and start exploring, analyzing, and visualizing it in Tableau.

2.4 Understanding data types in Tableau

In Tableau, understanding data types is essential as it affects how your data is interpreted, formatted, and visualized. This section will provide a detailed explanation of data types in Tableau, along with practical examples and step-by-step guidance on how to work with different data types.

Common Data Types in Tableau:

Tableau supports various data types to accommodate a wide range of data sources. Here are some of the common data types you'll encounter:

1. Dimension: Dimensions are categorical data types that define the attributes of your data. They are typically used to slice and dice data for analysis and visualization. Common dimension data types include:

- **String:** Textual data, such as product names or categories.

- **Date:** Date values, allowing for date-based analysis.

- **Geographical:** Geographic data, such as country or city names.

- **Boolean:** True or false values.

2. Measure: Measures are quantitative data types that can be aggregated, used in calculations, and visualized. They represent numerical values and include data types like:

- **Integer:** Whole numbers, such as quantities or counts.

- **Decimal:** Numeric values with decimal points, suitable for monetary amounts or percentages.

- **Currency:** Specialized data type for handling currency values.

- Percentage: A subtype of decimal used for percentage values.

Working with Data Types in Tableau:

Now, let's explore how to work with different data types in Tableau:

Step 1: Data Source Connection:

1. Start by connecting to your data source, whether it's an Excel file, a database, or any other data type.

2. During the connection, Tableau automatically assigns data types to the fields in your data source based on their content. However, you can modify these assignments as needed.

Step 2: Modifying Data Types:

1. To modify data types, select the field in the data pane, right-click it, and choose "Change Data Type."

2. You'll be presented with options to choose a different data type for the field. For example, you can change a field from "String" to "Date" if it represents a date.

Step 3: Handling Date Data:

1. Date fields in Tableau allow you to perform date-based analysis. By default, Tableau will recognize date values correctly. However, you can further refine date data by modifying formats.

2. To adjust date formats, right-click the date field, choose "Default Properties," and then "Date Format." You can select from a variety of date formats, or create custom ones.

Step 4: Handling Geographical Data:

1. When working with geographical data types, such as country names, it's essential to ensure Tableau recognizes the data as a geographical dimension.

2. Right-click the geographical field and choose "Geographic Role." You can specify whether it's a country, state, city, or other geographical dimension.

Step 5: Calculations with Data Types:

1. Tableau allows you to create calculated fields using various data types. For instance, you can perform mathematical calculations with numeric fields, or create date calculations with date fields.

2. To create calculated fields, click on "Analysis" in the menu bar, choose "Create Calculated Field," and follow the formula-building process.

Example: Modifying Data Types in Tableau

Let's say you have a dataset with a field named "OrderDate" that Tableau has recognized as a string data type. To change it to a date data type for proper date-based analysis:

1. Connect to your data source in Tableau.

2. In the data source tab, locate the "OrderDate" field in the data pane.

3. Right-click the "OrderDate" field and choose "Change Data Type."

4. Select the "Date" data type from the options.

5. Tableau will now interpret the "OrderDate" field as a date data type, allowing you to perform date-based calculations and visualizations.

In conclusion, understanding data types in Tableau is fundamental for accurate data analysis and visualization. Tableau automatically assigns data types to fields during data source connection, but you can modify these assignments to fit your specific needs. By adjusting data types, you can ensure that Tableau interprets and displays your data correctly, enabling you to create more accurate and informative visualizations.

CHAPTER III
Building Basic Charts, Graphs, and Visualizations

3.1 Using shelves for fields

In Tableau, shelves play a crucial role in building visualizations by allowing you to place and organize data fields to create charts, graphs, and other visual representations. This section will provide a detailed guide on how to use shelves effectively, including practical examples and step-by-step instructions.

Understanding the Shelves:

Tableau provides four primary shelves where you can place fields to define the structure and content of your visualizations:

1. Rows Shelf: This shelf defines the rows of your visualization. Placing a field in the Rows Shelf will generate separate rows in your chart for each distinct value in that field. For example, if you place a "Category" field in the Rows Shelf, you'll have one row for each product category.

2. Columns Shelf: The Columns Shelf defines the columns of your visualization. Fields placed in the Columns Shelf categorize and organize your data horizontally. For example, if you place a "Year" field in the Columns Shelf, you'll have separate columns for each year in your dataset.

3. Marks Card: The Marks Card allows you to define the level of detail, color, size, shape, and labels of the marks in your visualization. For instance, you can place a "Profit" field on the Marks Card to color your marks based on profit values.

4. Filters Shelf: The Filters Shelf is used to create data filters, which allow you to control the data displayed in your visualization. Fields placed in the Filters Shelf provide criteria for data inclusion or exclusion.

Using Shelves for Fields:

Let's go through the process of using shelves for fields to create a simple visualization in Tableau. For this example, we'll create a bar chart that shows the total sales of different product categories.

Step 1: Connect to Data:

1. Start by connecting to your data source in Tableau, whether it's a local file, database, or web data connector.

Step 2: Placing Fields in Shelves:

1. After connecting to your data, you'll see a list of available fields in the Data pane on the left.

2. To create a bar chart showing total sales by product category, drag and drop the following fields into the specified shelves:

  - Drag the "Product Category" field to the Rows Shelf.

  - Drag the "Sales" field to the Columns Shelf.

3. Tableau will automatically generate a bar chart displaying the total sales for each product category.

Step 3: Customizing the Visualization:

1. To further customize your visualization, you can use the Marks Card. For example, if you want to color the bars based on profit, drag the "Profit" field to the Color drop zone on the Marks Card.

2. You can also adjust the size, shape, and label options using the Marks Card.

Step 4: Formatting and Styling:

1. Use the toolbar to format and style your visualization. You can adjust colors, fonts, borders, and labels to make your visualization more appealing and informative.

Step 5: Interactivity and Filters:

1. If you want to add interactivity to your visualization, you can place additional fields in the Filters Shelf. For instance, you can allow users to filter the data by year or region.

2. By clicking on the filter, you can configure its settings and choose which fields to filter by.

Example: Creating a Bar Chart in Tableau:

In this example, we'll create a bar chart to visualize the total sales of different product categories in Tableau.

1. Connect to your data source in Tableau.

2. In the Data pane, drag the "Product Category" field to the Rows Shelf and the "Sales" field to the Columns Shelf.

3. Tableau will generate a bar chart.

4. To add interactivity, you can place additional fields in the Filters Shelf, such as "Year" to allow users to filter data by year.

In conclusion, using shelves for fields in Tableau is fundamental for building visualizations. By understanding the purpose of each shelf and how to place fields in them, you can create a wide range of charts, graphs, and visualizations that effectively convey insights from your data. The flexibility and interactivity provided by these shelves enable you to design meaningful and informative visualizations in Tableau.

3.2 Creating bar charts, line charts, and scatter plots

Tableau offers a diverse range of chart types to visualize data effectively. In this section, we will explore the creation of three fundamental chart types: bar charts, line charts, and scatter plots. We'll provide detailed instructions and practical examples to guide you through the process.

Creating Bar Charts:

Bar charts are excellent for comparing categorical data and displaying values across different categories. Follow these steps to create a bar chart in Tableau:

Step 1: Connect to Data:

1. Begin by connecting to your data source in Tableau.

Step 2: Placing Fields:

1. Drag and drop the desired dimension field to the "Columns Shelf." This field will determine the categories on the x-axis of your bar chart. For example, you could use a "Product Category" field.

2. Drag the measure field that you want to display on the y-axis to the "Rows Shelf." This field represents the values you want to compare, such as "Sales" or "Profit."

3. Tableau will automatically generate a vertical bar chart based on your selections.

Step 3: Customizing Bar Charts:

1. You can customize the appearance and behavior of your bar chart by using the "Marks Card."

2. For instance, you can color the bars based on a measure, adjust the size, and add labels to the bars using the "Label" card.

3. Use the "Format" option in the toolbar to further format and style your chart.

Creating Line Charts:

Line charts are used to visualize trends and changes in data over time or along an ordered dimension. Here's how to create a line chart in Tableau:

Step 1: Connect to Data:

1. Start by connecting to your data source in Tableau.

Step 2: Placing Fields:

1. Drag the dimension field that represents the time or ordered dimension to the "Columns Shelf."

2. Drag the measure field you want to track over time to the "Rows Shelf."

3. Tableau will create a line chart that shows the measure's trend over the ordered dimension.

Step 3: Customizing Line Charts:

1. Use the "Marks Card" to customize your line chart. You can adjust the appearance of lines, add labels, and color lines based on another measure.

2. Utilize the "Format" option in the toolbar to format and style your line chart.

Creating Scatter Plots:

Scatter plots are ideal for visualizing relationships between two continuous variables. Follow these steps to create a scatter plot in Tableau:

Step 1: Connect to Data:

1. Connect to your data source in Tableau.

Step 2: Placing Fields:

1. Drag one measure field to the "Columns Shelf." This field represents the x-axis of your scatter plot.

2. Drag another measure field to the "Rows Shelf." This field represents the y-axis of your scatter plot.

3. Tableau will generate a scatter plot, showing the relationship between the two measures.

Step 3: Customizing Scatter Plots:

1. Use the "Marks Card" to customize your scatter plot. You can adjust the size, color, shape, and labels of the data points based on dimensions or measures.

2. Access the "Format" option in the toolbar to format and style your scatter plot.

Examples: Creating Charts in Tableau:

Example 1: Bar Chart

Suppose you want to create a bar chart to visualize the total sales of different product categories. You'd follow the steps mentioned above, placing "Product Category" in the "Columns Shelf" and "Sales" in the "Rows Shelf."

Example 2: Line Chart

Imagine you have a dataset with monthly sales data and want to create a line chart to show the trend of sales over time. In this case, you'd place the date field in the "Columns Shelf" and the "Sales" field in the "Rows Shelf."

Example 3: Scatter Plot

Suppose you have a dataset with information on the height and weight of individuals, and you want to visualize the relationship between these two variables. You'd place the "Height" field in the "Columns Shelf" and the "Weight" field in the "Rows Shelf" to create a scatter plot.

In conclusion, Tableau provides a user-friendly interface for creating various chart types, including bar charts, line charts, and scatter plots. By following the steps and examples outlined in this section, you can efficiently visualize and analyze your data, enabling you to derive valuable insights and make data-driven decisions.

3.3 Building pie charts, maps, and tree maps

Tableau offers a wide range of visualization options, including pie charts, maps, and tree maps. In this section, we will explore how to create these specific chart types in Tableau, providing detailed instructions, practical examples, and step-by-step guidance.

Building Pie Charts:

Pie charts are useful for displaying the distribution of a single measure across different categories. Here's how to create a pie chart in Tableau:

Step 1: Connect to Data:

1. Begin by connecting to your data source in Tableau.

Step 2: Placing Fields:

1. Drag and drop the dimension field that defines your categories to the "Color" shelf on the "Marks Card."

2. Drag the measure field you want to represent in the pie chart to the "Angle" shelf on the "Marks Card."

3. Tableau will create a pie chart based on your selections.

Step 3: Customizing Pie Charts:

1. You can customize your pie chart using the "Marks Card." For example, you can add labels, adjust colors, and customize tooltips.

2. Utilize the "Format" option in the toolbar to further format and style your pie chart.

Building Maps:

Maps are essential for visualizing geographical data and showing data distribution across locations. Here's how to create a map in Tableau:

Step 1: Connect to Data:

1. Connect to your data source in Tableau, making sure it contains location data (latitude and longitude, city names, or postal codes).

Step 2: Placing Fields:

1. Drag the dimension field that represents the geographical dimension to the "Columns Shelf."

2. Drag the measure field that you want to visualize on the map to the "Rows Shelf."

3. Change the visualization type to "Map" by clicking on "Show Me" in the toolbar and selecting the map option.

4. Tableau will generate a map visualization, plotting your data points based on the geographical dimensions.

Step 3: Customizing Maps:

1. Customize your map using the "Marks Card." You can adjust the color, size, and label options of the data points.

2. Use the "Format" option in the toolbar to format and style your map, including map layers, background colors, and borders.

Building Tree Maps:

Tree maps are excellent for visualizing hierarchical data structures. Here's how to create a tree map in Tableau:

Step 1: Connect to Data:

1. Connect to your data source in Tableau, ensuring it contains hierarchical data, such as categories and subcategories.

Step 2: Placing Fields:

1. Drag the dimension fields representing the hierarchical structure to the "Rows Shelf." Typically, you'll have one field for the main category and another for subcategories.

2. Drag the measure field you want to represent in the tree map to the "Columns Shelf."

3. Tableau will create a tree map visualization, displaying hierarchical data with rectangles.

Step 3: Customizing Tree Maps:

1. Customize your tree map using the "Marks Card." You can adjust the size, color, and label options for the rectangles.

2. Use the "Format" option in the toolbar to format and style your tree map, including borders and shading.

Examples: Creating Charts and Visualizations in Tableau:

Example 1: Pie Chart

Suppose you want to create a pie chart to display the distribution of product categories in your dataset. Drag the "Product Category" dimension to the "Color" shelf and the "Sales" measure to the "Angle" shelf on the "Marks Card."

Example 2: Map

If you have a dataset containing location data, such as cities or coordinates, you can create a map to visualize data distribution across locations. Drag the geographical dimension (e.g., "City") to the "Columns Shelf" and the measure (e.g., "Sales") to the "Rows Shelf."

Example 3: Tree Map

Suppose you have hierarchical data, like categories and subcategories of products, and you want to create a tree map. Drag the dimension fields representing categories and subcategories to the "Rows Shelf" and the "Sales" measure to the "Columns Shelf."

In conclusion, Tableau offers a variety of visualization options, including pie charts, maps, and tree maps, to help you effectively represent and analyze your data. By following the steps and examples outlined in this section, you can create these specific chart types and enhance your data visualization capabilities in Tableau, making it easier to convey valuable insights to your audience.

3.4 Customizing and formatting visualizations

Creating clear and engaging visualizations is essential for effective data communication. In this section, we'll explore how to customize and format visualizations in Tableau to make them more informative and visually appealing. We'll provide practical examples and step-by-step instructions to guide you through the process.

Customizing and Formatting Bar Charts:

Bar charts are commonly used for comparing data across different categories. To customize and format a bar chart in Tableau, follow these steps:

Step 1: Create a Bar Chart:

1. Start by creating a bar chart, as described in Section 3.2.

Step 2: Customizing Colors:

1. To change the colors of the bars, click on the color legend on the "Marks Card."

2. You can choose from various color palettes or create a custom color scheme.

Step 3: Adding Labels:

1. To add data labels to the bars, click on the "Label" shelf on the "Marks Card."

2. You can customize the label format, font size, and color.

Step 4: Adjusting Bar Size:

1. You can change the width of the bars by adjusting the "Size" shelf on the "Marks Card."

Step 5: Formatting Axes:

1. To format the axes, right-click on the axis and choose "Format."

2. You can customize axis labels, tick marks, and scaling options.

Step 6: Adding Tooltips:

1. To provide additional information when users hover over the bars, customize the tooltips.

2. Click on the "Tooltip" shelf on the "Marks Card" to edit the tooltip content.

Customizing and Formatting Line Charts:

Line charts are ideal for showing trends over time or along an ordered dimension. To customize and format a line chart in Tableau, follow these steps:

Step 1: Create a Line Chart:

1. Start by creating a line chart, as described in Section 3.2.

Step 2: Customizing Lines:

1. To change the appearance of lines, click on the line legend on the "Marks Card."

2. You can adjust line thickness, style, and color.

Step 3: Adding Data Points:

1. You can add data points to your line chart by clicking on the "Circle" shelf on the "Marks Card."

Step 4: Formatting Axes:

1. Format the axes as described in the bar chart customization section.

Step 5: Adding Tooltips:

1. Customize the tooltips to provide relevant information when users hover over the data points.

Customizing and Formatting Maps:

Maps are useful for visualizing geographical data. To customize and format a map in Tableau, follow these steps:

Step 1: Create a Map:

1. Start by creating a map, as described in Section 3.3.

Step 2: Customizing Data Points:

1. To change the appearance of data points on the map, click on the "Circle" shelf on the "Marks Card."

2. You can adjust the size, color, and shape of data points.

Step 3: Customizing Map Layers:

1. Customize map layers, such as background color, labels, and borders, using the "Format" option in the toolbar.

Step 4: Adding Tooltips:

1. Customize the tooltips to provide location-specific information when users hover over data points on the map.

Customizing and Formatting Tree Maps:

Tree maps are great for visualizing hierarchical data. To customize and format a tree map in Tableau, follow these steps:

Step 1: Create a Tree Map:

1. Start by creating a tree map, as described in Section 3.3.

Step 2: Customizing Rectangles:

1. To change the appearance of rectangles in the tree map, click on the "Rectangle" shelf on the "Marks Card."

2. You can adjust the size, color, and label options for the rectangles.

Step 3: Adding Labels:

1. You can add labels to the rectangles by clicking on the "Label" shelf on the "Marks Card."

Step 4: Formatting Borders:

1. To format the borders of rectangles, use the "Format" option in the toolbar.

Examples: Customizing and Formatting Visualizations in Tableau:

Example 1: Bar Chart Customization:

Suppose you've created a bar chart showing sales by product category. To customize and format it, you can change the colors of the bars, add labels, adjust the bar size, and format the axes.

Example 2: Line Chart Customization:

If you've created a line chart to display monthly revenue, you can customize it by changing the line styles and colors, adding data points, and formatting the axes.

Example 3: Map Customization:

Suppose you've created a map to visualize store locations. You can customize it by changing the appearance of data points, formatting map layers, and enhancing tooltips.

Example 4: Tree Map Customization:

If you've created a tree map to represent product sales within categories and subcategories, you can customize it by adjusting the rectangle sizes, adding labels, and formatting borders.

In summary, customizing and formatting visualizations in Tableau is crucial for creating visually appealing and informative representations of your data. By following the steps and examples provided in this section, you can enhance your data visualizations to effectively convey insights and engage your audience.

3.5 Creating dashboards and storytelling

In Tableau, dashboards and storytelling are powerful features that allow you to combine multiple visualizations and present your data in a compelling and interactive manner. This section will guide you through the process of creating dashboards and storytelling in Tableau, providing detailed instructions and practical examples.

Creating Dashboards:

Dashboards in Tableau are interactive canvases where you can combine multiple visualizations and present them in a unified view. Here's how to create a dashboard:

Step 1: Create Visualizations:

1. Start by creating the visualizations you want to include in your dashboard. This could be a combination of bar charts, line charts, maps, or any other visualization types.

Step 2: Build a Dashboard:

1. From the "Dashboard" menu, select "New Dashboard."

2. This will open the dashboard canvas, and you can start adding sheets (visualizations) by dragging them from the "Sheets" tab.

3. Arrange the sheets on the dashboard canvas and adjust their size and layout as needed.

Step 3: Add Interactivity:

1. To make your dashboard interactive, you can add filter actions, highlight actions, URL actions, or parameter actions. These actions allow users to interact with the dashboard and see how different selections affect the visualizations.

Step 4: Customize the Dashboard:

1. Customize the dashboard by adding a title, adjusting formatting, and setting the dashboard size to fit different devices.

Creating Storytelling:

Storytelling in Tableau allows you to create a sequence of sheets and dashboards that guide your audience through a data-driven narrative. Here's how to create storytelling in Tableau:

Step 1: Create Sheets and Dashboards:

1. Start by creating the visualizations and dashboards you want to include in your story.

Step 2: Build a Story:

1. From the "Story" menu, select "New Story."

2. This will open the storytelling canvas, where you can start adding sheets and dashboards.

3. Arrange the sheets and dashboards in the desired sequence to create a narrative flow.

Step 3: Add Captions and Annotations:

1. Enhance your storytelling by adding captions and annotations to explain the data and insights to your audience.

Step 4: Customize the Story:

1. Customize the story by setting the size, theme, and navigation options. You can also add a cover page to introduce your story.

Examples: Creating Dashboards and Storytelling in Tableau:

Example 1: Dashboard Creation:

Suppose you have multiple visualizations, including a bar chart showing sales by product category and a map showing store locations. To create a dashboard, you can combine these visualizations on a single canvas, allowing users to explore the data interactively.

Example 2: Storytelling:

Imagine you want to tell a data-driven story about sales performance over the past year. You can create a story that begins with an overview dashboard, followed by interactive visualizations showing monthly trends, regional breakdowns, and product category analysis. Each step in the story guides the audience through the narrative.

In summary, Tableau's dashboards and storytelling features enable you to present your data in an engaging and informative way. By following the steps and examples outlined in this section, you can effectively create dashboards and stories that help your audience understand and connect with the data, making it easier to convey valuable insights and make data-driven decisions.

CHAPTER IV
Data Preparation and Transformation

4.1 Using Tableau Prep for Data Preparation

Introduction to Tableau Prep

Tableau Prep is a powerful tool for data preparation and transformation, allowing you to clean, shape, and enrich your data before creating visualizations in Tableau Desktop. In this section, we'll provide an in-depth introduction to Tableau Prep, explaining its key features and how to use it effectively.

Understanding Tableau Prep:

Tableau Prep is a data preparation tool that simplifies and streamlines the process of cleaning, reshaping, and combining data from various sources. It provides a user-friendly interface for data engineers, analysts, and data scientists to perform the following tasks:

- Data Connection: Connect to various data sources, such as databases, spreadsheets, and web data connectors.

- Data Profiling: Understand the quality and structure of your data through data profiling, which helps identify issues like missing values, duplicate records, and data types.

- **Data Cleaning:** Cleanse and transform your data by handling missing values, correcting data types, and removing or replacing outliers.

- **Data Shaping:** Pivot, split, and aggregate data to make it suitable for analysis. You can also combine data from different sources using data joining and blending.

- **Data Validation:** Validate data against predefined business rules to ensure data quality and consistency.

- **Output Options:** Tableau Prep allows you to output your cleaned and transformed data to various destinations, including Tableau Desktop, Tableau Server, and other data storage systems.

Using Tableau Prep:

Let's explore how to use Tableau Prep for data preparation:

Step 1: Connecting to Data:

1. Launch Tableau Prep and start a new workflow.

2. Connect to your data source by selecting the appropriate connector. You can connect to databases, cloud data sources, flat files, and more.

Step 2: Profiling and Exploring Data:

1. Once you've connected to your data, Tableau Prep will automatically profile it. You can view data quality insights, such as data type distributions, missing values, and unique values.

Step 3: Cleaning Data:

1. Begin cleaning your data by addressing issues like missing values, outliers, and incorrect data types. You can use drag-and-drop operations to clean data easily.

Step 4: Shaping Data:

1. Shape your data using various operations like pivoting, splitting, aggregating, and joining tables. These operations are performed in a visual, intuitive interface.

Step 5: Validating Data:

1. Define validation rules to ensure data quality and consistency. Tableau Prep will flag data that doesn't meet your defined criteria.

Step 6: Output Data:

1. Once your data is cleaned and transformed to your satisfaction, you can output it to a destination of your choice, such as a Tableau data source or a database.

Benefits of Using Tableau Prep:

- **Data Integrity:** Tableau Prep helps ensure data accuracy and consistency by identifying and addressing data quality issues.

- **Time Savings:** By providing a user-friendly interface and automated data profiling, Tableau Prep reduces the time spent on data preparation tasks.

- **Data Exploration:** The profiling capabilities allow you to gain insights into your data, making it easier to understand its structure and quality.

- **Data Collaboration:** You can save your Tableau Prep workflows and share them with others for collaborative data preparation.

- **Seamless Integration:** Tableau Prep seamlessly integrates with Tableau Desktop and Tableau Server, making it easy to move from data preparation to data visualization.

Example: Using Tableau Prep for Data Preparation:

Suppose you have a dataset containing customer information with missing values, inconsistent date formats, and data discrepancies. You can use Tableau Prep to connect to the data source, clean missing values, standardize date formats, and validate data against defined business rules. Once the data is prepared, you can output it to Tableau Desktop for creating meaningful visualizations.

In conclusion, Tableau Prep is a valuable tool for data preparation and transformation, providing a user-friendly interface and automation to ensure data quality and accuracy. By following the steps and examples outlined in this section, you can harness the power of Tableau Prep to clean, shape, and enrich your data, setting the stage for impactful data visualization and analysis.

Cleaning, shaping, and transforming data

Data preparation is a crucial step in the data analysis process, as raw data often contains errors, inconsistencies, and the need for restructuring. Tableau Prep is a powerful tool that simplifies the process of cleaning, shaping, and transforming your data. In this section, we will walk through a real-world example to demonstrate how to use Tableau Prep effectively for data preparation.

Example: Cleaning, Shaping, and Transforming Data

Scenario: You work for a retail company, and you have received a dataset containing sales data. The dataset is messy, with missing values, duplicate records, and a need for data reshaping. Your goal is to clean the data, shape it for analysis, and transform it to calculate the profit margin.

Step 1: Connecting to Data

1. Launch Tableau Prep and create a new workflow.

2. Connect to your data source by selecting the appropriate connector, whether it's a CSV file, an Excel spreadsheet, or a database. In our case, we have a CSV file containing the sales data.

Step 2: Data Profiling

1. Once you've connected to the data, Tableau Prep will automatically profile it, providing insights into the data's quality. In this example, you discover that there are missing values in the "Profit" and "Discount" columns, and some records are duplicates.

2. You identify the following issues:

   - Missing values in the "Profit" and "Discount" columns.

   - Duplicate records.

Step 3: Cleaning Data

Cleaning Missing Values:

1. Address the missing values in the "Profit" and "Discount" columns by applying imputation. In Tableau Prep, you can use the "Clean" step to do this. For the "Profit" column, you choose to impute missing values with the average profit. For the "Discount" column, you decide to impute missing values with zero, assuming no discount for missing values.

Handling Duplicate Records:

2. To handle duplicate records, use the "Clean" step to remove duplicates based on specific columns. In our case, we'll remove duplicates based on the "Order ID" column.

Step 4: Shaping Data

Pivoting Data:

1. Now, let's shape the data. In our dataset, the "Region" and "Category" columns are represented as separate columns for each year. To reshape this data for easier analysis, you can use the "Pivot" step. Pivot the data for "Region" and "Category" columns, creating new columns for each year with the corresponding values.

Step 5: Transforming Data

Calculating Profit Margin:

1. To transform the data, you want to calculate the profit margin as a percentage. In Tableau Prep, you can use the "Add Calculation" step. Create a new calculated field named "Profit Margin" and define the calculation as "(Profit / Sales) 100" to calculate the profit margin as a percentage.

2. The data is now transformed to include the profit margin, making it more insightful for analysis.

Step 6: Review and Output Data

1. Review the data to ensure it's clean, shaped, and transformed as per your requirements.

2. You can now output this clean, structured, and transformed dataset to various destinations, including a Tableau data source, for further analysis and visualization.

By following these steps and addressing the data quality issues, you have successfully prepared and transformed the dataset, making it suitable for meaningful analysis and visualizations.

In summary, Tableau Prep simplifies the data preparation process by offering an intuitive interface for cleaning, shaping, and transforming data. This example demonstrates how to tackle real-world data challenges and leverage Tableau Prep to ensure data accuracy and relevance for your analytics tasks.

.

Combining and pivoting data tables

Data preparation often involves the need to combine and reshape data tables to create a more structured and analyzable dataset. Tableau Prep provides powerful tools to achieve this. In this section, we'll walk through an example of how to combine and pivot data tables using Tableau Prep.

Example: Combining and Pivoting Data Tables

Scenario: You work for a retail company, and you have two separate datasets. One contains sales data by product, and the other contains sales data by region. Your goal is to combine these datasets and pivot the data to create a single dataset for analysis.

Step 1: Connecting to Data

1. Launch Tableau Prep and create a new workflow.

2. Connect to your first dataset, which contains sales data by product, and add it to the workflow. You can use a CSV file, Excel spreadsheet, or other data sources.

3. Similarly, connect to your second dataset, which contains sales data by region, and add it to the workflow.

Step 2: Combining Data Tables

1. To combine the two datasets, use the "Clean" step in Tableau Prep.

2. In the "Clean" step, choose the first dataset (sales data by product) and add a join clause to specify how it should be combined with the second dataset (sales data by region). In this example, you might use a common field like "Product ID" or "Region" to establish the connection.

3. Configure the join type (e.g., inner, left, right, full outer) based on your data integration requirements. Ensure that you select the appropriate join condition and resolve any conflicts.

4. This step combines the two datasets into a single, unified dataset that includes product-related and region-related information.

Step 3: Pivoting Data

1. Now that you have a combined dataset, you need to pivot the data to make it more suitable for analysis. In this example, we'll pivot the data to show sales figures by product category and region.

2. Use the "Pivot" step in Tableau Prep.

3. Select the columns you want to pivot. In this case, you might select columns related to different product categories and regions.

4. Configure the pivot settings, specifying the pivot field (e.g., "Category" and "Region"), and the aggregated values (e.g., "Sales").

5. The data is now transformed, with the pivoted columns representing different product categories and regions.

Step 4: Review and Output Data

1. Review the combined and pivoted dataset to ensure it aligns with your analysis goals.

2. Once you're satisfied with the data structure, you can output it to a destination of your choice, such as a Tableau data source, for further analysis, and visualization.

By following these steps, you have successfully combined and pivoted your data tables, creating a unified dataset that is more amenable to analysis and reporting.

In summary, Tableau Prep's ability to combine and pivot data tables simplifies the process of preparing data for analysis. This example demonstrates how to address the challenge of integrating and reshaping data from different sources to create a single, structured dataset, ready for meaningful analysis and visualization.

4.2 Data Joining, Blending, and Aggregations

Understanding data relationships

In data analysis, understanding data relationships is a fundamental concept. It involves recognizing how different datasets are related and how they can be combined for a more comprehensive analysis. In this section, we will explore the notion of data relationships and provide a practical example of how to understand and work with them.

Example: Understanding Data Relationships

Scenario: You are working with a retail company that has two datasets. The first dataset contains information about customer orders, including order details and customer information. The second dataset contains product information, such as product names, categories, and prices. Your goal is to understand the data relationships between these two datasets to analyze customer purchasing behavior.

Step 1: Connecting to Data

1. Begin by launching Tableau Prep and creating a new workflow.

2. Connect to your first dataset, which contains customer order information, and add it to the workflow. You can use a data source like a database, CSV file, or Excel spreadsheet.

3. Similarly, connect to your second dataset, which contains product information, and add it to the workflow.

Step 2: Understanding Data Relationships

1. To understand the data relationships between these two datasets, you need to identify common fields or keys that can serve as a bridge between them. Common fields can include unique identifiers such as order IDs, customer IDs, or product IDs.

2. In this example, you might notice that both datasets have an "Order ID" field. This field can serve as a key to establish a relationship between the two datasets.

3. Analyze the data structure to understand how the "Order ID" field is structured and whether it's consistent in both datasets. Ensure that the data types and values match for this field.

Step 3: Data Joining

1. Once you've identified a common field (e.g., "Order ID"), you can use the "Join" step in Tableau Prep to combine the datasets based on this field.

2. Configure the join type (inner, left, right, full outer) based on your analysis needs. In this case, an inner join ensures that you only include records with matching "Order ID" values in both datasets.

3. Specify the join condition by selecting the "Order ID" field from both datasets. You can also select additional fields for your analysis.

Step 4: Aggregations and Analysis

1. After joining the datasets, you now have a unified dataset that combines customer order information with product information. You can use this dataset for various analysis and aggregations.

2. For example, you can calculate the total sales, average order value, or product preferences based on this combined dataset.

3. You can also create visualizations and dashboards in Tableau to gain insights into customer purchasing behavior.

Step 5: Review and Output Data

1. Carefully review the joined dataset to ensure it aligns with your analysis objectives.

2. Once you are satisfied with the data structure and relationships, you can output it to a destination of your choice for further analysis and reporting.

Understanding data relationships is key to integrating datasets effectively and deriving valuable insights from your data. By following these steps and recognizing the connections between datasets, you can conduct more comprehensive analyses and make data-driven decisions.

In summary, data relationships play a pivotal role in data analysis, and Tableau Prep provides a user-friendly platform for joining and exploring these relationships, allowing for a deeper understanding of your data and more informed decision-making.

Performing joins, unions, and cross-database joins

Data analysis often requires combining data from various sources, which can be achieved through joins, unions, and cross-database joins. In this section, we'll explore these data integration techniques using Tableau, providing practical examples and step-by-step guidance.

Example: Performing Joins, Unions, and Cross-Database Joins

Scenario: You are a data analyst working with a retail company. You have two datasets: one containing customer order details and another with product sales information. You also need to combine data from a third-party survey tool for customer feedback. Your goal is to integrate these datasets for a comprehensive analysis.

Step 1: Connecting to Data

1. Start by opening Tableau and creating a new workbook.

2. Connect to your first dataset, the one containing customer order details. You can connect to data sources like databases, spreadsheets, or cloud storage.

3. Similarly, connect to your second dataset, which includes product sales information.

4. If your customer feedback data resides in a separate database, connect to it as well.

Step 2: Performing Joins

1. In Tableau, use the "Data Source" tab to see all the datasets you've connected to.

2. To perform a join, select the primary dataset, usually the one you want to build your analysis around. In this example, you might choose the customer order details dataset.

3. Drag the second dataset, the product sales information, onto the primary dataset. Tableau will prompt you to specify the join type (e.g., inner, left, right, full outer). Choose the appropriate type for your analysis.

4. Define the join condition by selecting common fields between the two datasets. In this case, you might choose "Order ID" as the key.

5. Tableau will perform the join and create a unified dataset based on your specifications.

Step 3: Unions

1. Unions are useful when you need to combine data vertically, i.e., stacking data on top of each other. In Tableau, you can perform unions on datasets with similar structures.

2. To perform a union, navigate to the "Data Source" tab and select one of the datasets.

3. Drag and drop the second dataset onto the first one while holding down the Ctrl key (or Command key on Mac).

4. Tableau will prompt you to confirm the union. Ensure that the field mappings are correct.

5. Tableau will create a single dataset by stacking the rows from both datasets.

Step 4: Cross-Database Joins

1. Cross-database joins allow you to integrate data from different database platforms. In Tableau, you can join tables from different databases.

2. From the "Data Source" tab, ensure that you have connected to data from the different databases.

3. Choose the primary dataset and drag the secondary dataset from another database onto it.

4. Define the join type and conditions as you would with regular joins.

5. Tableau will perform the cross-database join and create a unified dataset for your analysis.

Step 5: Review and Build Analysis

1. Review the integrated dataset to ensure it aligns with your analysis goals.

2. You can now proceed to build your analysis, create visualizations, and extract insights from the combined data.

Step 6: Output Data

1. Once you've conducted your analysis, you can output the results to various destinations, such as Tableau workbooks, databases, or files.

By following these steps and performing joins, unions, and cross-database joins in Tableau, you can seamlessly integrate data from various sources, enabling a more comprehensive and insightful analysis of your data.

In summary, Tableau provides a versatile platform for combining and integrating data from multiple sources, offering the flexibility to work with data efficiently, regardless of its origin.

Using data blending to combine multiple data sources

Data blending is a powerful technique in Tableau that allows you to combine data from multiple sources or datasets seamlessly. In this section, we'll explore data blending in Tableau, providing a practical example and step-by-step guidance.

Example: Using Data Blending in Tableau

Scenario: You are a data analyst working for a retail company. You have two datasets: one containing sales data and another with customer demographic information. Both datasets share a common field, such as "Customer ID." Your goal is to blend these datasets to analyze sales trends by customer demographics.

Step 1: Connecting to Data

1. Start by launching Tableau and creating a new workbook.

2. Connect to your primary dataset, which contains sales data, and add it to your workbook. You can connect to data sources like databases, spreadsheets, or cloud storage.

3. Next, connect to your secondary dataset, which includes customer demographic information.

Step 2: Data Blending

1. In Tableau, navigate to the primary dataset and create a new worksheet.

2. Drag a field from the primary dataset (e.g., "Customer ID") to your Rows or Columns shelf.

3. From the secondary dataset, drag the corresponding field ("Customer ID") to your Rows or Columns shelf as well.

4. Tableau will automatically detect the relationship between these two fields and blend the data.

Step 3: Building the Analysis

1. Now that your data is blended, you can start building your analysis. For example, you can create visualizations, like bar charts, line charts, or scatter plots, to analyze sales trends by customer demographics.

2. Drag fields from the primary and secondary datasets to the Marks card to differentiate your analysis based on customer demographics.

3. You can also use calculated fields to perform custom calculations that involve blended data.

Step 4: Review and Output Data

1. Carefully review your analysis to ensure it aligns with your objectives.

2. Once you are satisfied with your analysis, you can output the results to various destinations, such as Tableau workbooks, dashboards, or images.

Step 5: Data Cleanup and Transformation

1. It's essential to ensure that the data in both datasets align correctly for successful data blending. Data cleaning and transformation may be necessary to address inconsistencies or discrepancies.

2. Use Tableau Prep or other data preparation tools to clean and shape your data.

Step 6: Resolving Data Conflicts

1. Data blending may introduce conflicts if there are inconsistent or missing data in your datasets. In Tableau, you can resolve data conflicts by setting up data source filters or using data source options.

2. Address issues like null values, duplicate records, or data mismatches.

Step 7: Advanced Data Blending

1. In more complex scenarios, you can use the Data menu in Tableau to access advanced data blending options, such as data source filtering, data source options, and data relationships.

2. These options allow for fine-tuning the blending process, especially when dealing with multiple data sources.

By following these steps and using data blending in Tableau, you can seamlessly combine data from multiple sources to conduct in-depth analysis and gain insights. This technique allows you to leverage the strengths of different datasets and produce a more comprehensive view of your data.

In summary, data blending in Tableau is a valuable feature for data analysts and professionals seeking to integrate and analyze data from multiple sources effectively. It offers a user-friendly approach to blending data and extracting meaningful insights.

Aggregating and summarizing data for analysis

Aggregating and summarizing data is a fundamental step in data preparation and transformation. It involves condensing large datasets into more manageable forms, such as averages, totals, or counts, to facilitate analysis. In this section, we'll explore how to aggregate and summarize data in Tableau, providing a practical example and step-by-step guidance.

Example: Aggregating and Summarizing Data in Tableau

Scenario: You work for a marketing department and have a dataset containing daily website traffic data. You want to summarize this data to identify monthly trends in website visits.

Step 1: Connecting to Data

1. Begin by opening Tableau and creating a new workbook.

2. Connect to your dataset, which contains daily website traffic data. The dataset should include fields like "Date," "Page Views," and "Visitors."

Step 2: Aggregating Data for Monthly Analysis

1. Create a new worksheet in Tableau.

2. Drag the "Date" field to the Columns shelf. Tableau may automatically set this as a continuous date axis.

3. To summarize data by month, right-click on the "Date" field and select "Month" under the "Date Properties."

4. Drag the "Page Views" field to the Rows shelf.

5. Tableau will automatically aggregate data by month, giving you the total page views for each month.

6. To view monthly unique visitors, drag the "Visitors" field to the Rows shelf as well.

Step 3: Custom Aggregations

1. In some cases, you may need custom aggregations, such as calculating the average page views per visitor per month.

2. To create a custom aggregation, right-click in the Rows shelf and choose "Measure" > "Create Calculated Field."

3. Write a calculated field formula, such as [Page Views] / [Visitors], and give it a meaningful name.

4. Drag the custom aggregation to the Rows shelf to include it in your analysis.

Step 4: Using Aggregation Functions

1. Tableau provides various aggregation functions like SUM, AVG, COUNT, and more.

2. To use these functions, simply drag a field to the Rows or Columns shelf, and then click the drop-down arrow next to the field. Choose the aggregation function you want to apply.

Step 5: Building Visualizations

1. After aggregating and summarizing the data, you can create visualizations like line charts, bar charts, or area charts to visualize the trends and insights.

2. Drag fields to the Marks card to differentiate your analysis further.

Step 6: Filtering and Sorting

1. Use filters and sorting options to refine your analysis. For instance, you can filter data for specific time ranges or sort the data by a particular metric.

Step 7: Review and Output Data

1. Carefully review your aggregated and summarized data to ensure it aligns with your analysis objectives.

2. Output your results in Tableau worksheets, dashboards, or reports for presentation or further analysis.

Step 8: Additional Data Transformation

If you need additional data transformation, such as pivoting, cleaning, or handling missing data, you can utilize Tableau Prep or other data preparation tools.

By following these steps and using Tableau's aggregation and summarization capabilities, you can effectively condense large datasets and gain valuable insights from your data. Whether you're examining trends, calculating averages, or deriving custom aggregations, Tableau provides the tools to streamline your data analysis process.

In summary, aggregating and summarizing data is a crucial part of data preparation and transformation in Tableau. These techniques enable you to make sense of complex datasets and extract meaningful insights for better decision-making.

4.3 Data Filtering, Sorting, and Grouping

Applying data filters for data reduction

Data filtering is a crucial process in data preparation, as it allows you to focus on specific subsets of data that are relevant to your analysis. In Tableau, you can apply various types of filters to reduce data and extract valuable insights. In this section, we'll explore how to apply data filters in Tableau, providing a practical example and step-by-step guidance.

Example: Applying Data Filters in Tableau

Scenario: You have a large dataset containing sales data for multiple product categories, and you want to filter the data to focus on a specific product category for analysis.

Step 1: Connecting to Data

1. Open Tableau and create a new workbook.

2. Connect to your dataset, which contains sales data. Ensure the dataset includes fields like "Product Category," "Sales," and "Date."

Step 2: Adding Data to the Worksheet

1. Create a new worksheet in Tableau.

2. Drag the "Product Category" field to the Columns shelf.

3. Drag the "Sales" field to the Rows shelf.

4. Tableau will automatically create a visualization that displays sales data for all product categories.

Step 3: Applying Data Filters

1. To apply a data filter, you can use the following methods:

   - Drag the "Product Category" field to the "Filters" shelf.

   - Right-click on a specific product category in the visualization and select "Filter."

2. Tableau will create a filter card where you can select which product categories to include in your analysis.

3. You can choose multiple categories or even apply more advanced conditions if needed.

Step 4: Review and Output Data

1. Carefully review the filtered data and ensure it aligns with your analysis goals.

2. Output your filtered results to Tableau worksheets, dashboards, or reports for further exploration or presentation.

Step 5: Interactive Data Filtering

1. Tableau provides interactive data filtering options, allowing users to adjust filters dynamically in dashboards.

2. To implement interactive filters, create a dashboard and add filter actions that link different worksheets.

3. This enables users to interactively filter data while exploring visualizations.

Step 6: Combining Filters

1. You can combine multiple filters to refine your data reduction. For example, you may filter by both product category and date range to focus on specific data subsets.

2. Be cautious not to overfilter, as it might limit your analysis options.

Step 7: Advanced Filtering Options

1. Tableau offers advanced filtering options, such as data source filters, context filters, and top N filters.

2. Data source filters allow you to filter data at the source level, reducing the amount of data loaded into Tableau.

3. Context filters create a subset of data that other filters act upon, allowing for more complex filtering logic.

4. Top N filters help you identify the top or bottom values in a specific metric.

Step 8: Review and Adjust Filters

1. Regularly review and adjust your filters to ensure they align with your evolving analysis objectives.

2. Filters can be modified or removed as needed.

By following these steps and utilizing the filtering capabilities in Tableau, you can effectively reduce data to focus on specific subsets and gain valuable insights. Data filtering is a dynamic process that allows you to analyze the most relevant information, making it an essential part of data analysis.

In summary, applying data filters in Tableau is a powerful technique for reducing data and concentrating on specific subsets that are pertinent to your analysis. Whether you're filtering by categories, date ranges, or using more advanced filtering options, Tableau provides the tools to extract meaningful insights from your data.

Sorting data for better visualization

Sorting data is an important step in data preparation and analysis, as it allows you to arrange your data in a meaningful and visually appealing way. In Tableau, you can sort data to improve visualization and make your insights more accessible. In this section, we'll explore how to sort data in Tableau, providing a practical example and step-by-step guidance.

Example: Sorting Data in Tableau

Scenario: You have a dataset containing sales data for multiple products, and you want to sort the products by their sales values in descending order for a bar chart.

Step 1: Connecting to Data

1. Open Tableau and create a new workbook.

2. Connect to your dataset, which contains sales data. Ensure the dataset includes fields like "Product Name" and "Sales."

Step 2: Adding Data to the Worksheet

1. Create a new worksheet in Tableau.

2. Drag the "Product Name" field to the Columns shelf.

3. Drag the "Sales" field to the Rows shelf.

4. Tableau will create a bar chart displaying the products and their respective sales values.

Step 3: Sorting Data

1. To sort the data in descending order by sales values, you can follow these steps:

  - Click on the "Sales" axis in your visualization to select it.

- Click the drop-down arrow on the axis, and from the menu, select "Sort."

- In the "Sort" dialog box, choose "Descending" and click "OK."

2. Your data will now be sorted in descending order based on sales values.

Step 4: Additional Sorting Options

1. Tableau provides various sorting options, including sorting by dimensions, measures, or even custom sorting.

2. To sort by a dimension, you can right-click on a dimension in your visualization and select "Sort" to arrange it alphabetically or by another criterion.

3. For custom sorting, you can create a calculated field that assigns custom sorting values to your data.

Step 5: Review and Output Data

1. Carefully review the sorted data and ensure it enhances your visualization and analysis.

2. Output your sorted results in Tableau worksheets, dashboards, or reports for presentation or further exploration.

Step 6: Interactive Sorting

1. Tableau allows for interactive sorting, which means end-users can adjust sorting dynamically in dashboards.

2. To enable interactive sorting, create a dashboard and add sort actions to your visualizations.

3. This empowers users to change the sorting criteria to suit their preferences.

Step 7: Sorting for Clarity

1. Sorting data is essential for visual clarity and understanding. It helps you emphasize key insights and relationships.

2. In some cases, you may need to sort data by multiple dimensions or measures to create effective visualizations.

Step 8: Review and Adjust Sorting

1. Regularly review and adjust your sorting options as your analysis evolves.

2. Sorting can be modified or removed based on your analysis goals.

By following these steps and using Tableau's sorting capabilities, you can enhance the clarity and impact of your data visualizations. Whether you're sorting by measures, dimensions, or applying custom sorting, Tableau provides the tools to make your insights more accessible and compelling.

In summary, sorting data in Tableau is a critical aspect of data visualization and analysis. It enables you to arrange data in a meaningful way, highlighting key insights and making your visualizations more informative and visually appealing

Grouping data to create hierarchical views

Grouping data in Tableau is a valuable technique that enables you to organize and present your data in a hierarchical or categorized manner, making it easier for users to explore and understand the information. In this section, we'll explore how to group data in Tableau, providing a practical example and step-by-step guidance.

Example: Grouping Data in Tableau

Scenario: You have a dataset with sales data for various products, and you want to create a hierarchical view by grouping products into categories.

Step 1: Connecting to Data

1. Open Tableau and create a new workbook.

2. Connect to your dataset, which should include fields like "Product Name," "Category," and "Sales."

Step 2: Adding Data to the Worksheet

1. Create a new worksheet in Tableau.

2. Drag the "Product Name" field to the Rows shelf.

3. Drag the "Sales" field to the Columns shelf.

4. Tableau will create a basic bar chart displaying products and their sales values.

Step 3: Grouping Data

1. To group data based on product categories, follow these steps:

   - In the "Data" pane on the left, right-click on the "Product Name" field.

   - Select "Create" and then choose "Group."

   - In the "Group" dialog, select the products you want to group under specific categories. For example, select "Electronics" for all electronic products.

   - You can repeat this process for each product category.

2. Tableau will create a new dimension that represents your grouped categories.

Step 4: Creating Hierarchical Views

1. To create a hierarchical view, you can drag the grouped category dimension (e.g., "Category") to the Rows shelf before the "Product Name" field.

2. This will create a hierarchy, allowing you to drill down from categories to individual products.

Step 5: Customizing and Formatting

1. You can customize the appearance of your hierarchical view by adding labels, adjusting colors, and formatting.

2. You can also create a dashboard that includes filter actions to make the hierarchical view interactive.

Step 6: Review and Output Data

1. Carefully review your grouped and hierarchical view to ensure it meets your analysis objectives.

2. Output your hierarchical results in Tableau worksheets, dashboards, or reports for presentation or exploration.

Step 7: Advanced Grouping Options

1. Tableau offers advanced grouping options, such as combined fields, calculated fields, and more complex logic for grouping.

2. You can create calculated fields that define custom grouping rules based on your specific requirements.

Step 8: Review and Adjust Grouping

1. Regularly review and adjust your grouping as your analysis evolves.

2. Grouping can be modified, and new groupings can be created to adapt to changing needs.

By following these steps and using Tableau's grouping capabilities, you can create hierarchical views that provide a structured and intuitive way to explore your data. Grouping is particularly valuable when you want to present data in categories or hierarchies that make sense to your audience.

In summary, grouping data in Tableau allows you to organize and present your data in a hierarchical manner, enhancing the user's ability to explore and understand the information. Whether you're grouping by categories, creating custom hierarchies, or using calculated fields for advanced grouping, Tableau offers the tools to present your data effectively.

Applying sets and groups for data organization

In Tableau, sets and groups are powerful tools for organizing and analyzing data. Sets allow you to create custom subsets of data based on specific conditions, while groups enable you to categorize and structure your data for more effective analysis. In this section, we'll explore how to apply sets and groups in Tableau with a practical example.

Example: Applying Sets and Groups in Tableau

Scenario: You have a dataset containing sales data for various products and want to create a set to highlight top-performing products and a group to categorize products by profitability.

Step 1: Connecting to Data

1. Open Tableau and create a new workbook.

2. Connect to your dataset, which should include fields like "Product Name," "Sales," and "Profit."

Step 2: Adding Data to the Worksheet

1. Create a new worksheet in Tableau.

2. Drag the "Product Name" field to the Rows shelf.

3. Drag the "Sales" field to the Columns shelf.

4. Tableau will create a basic bar chart displaying products and their sales values.

Step 3: Creating a Set for Top-Performing Products

1. To create a set for top-performing products, follow these steps:

  - In the "Data" pane on the left, right-click on the "Sales" field.

  - Select "Create" and then choose "Set."

  - In the "Create Set" dialog, specify your set's conditions. For example, you can set the top 10 products based on sales.

- Name your set, e.g., "Top Products."

2. Tableau will create a set that includes the top-performing products based on your conditions.

Step 4: Highlighting Top Products

1. To highlight the top products in your worksheet, drag the "Top Products" set to the Color shelf.

2. This will color the bars representing the top products differently.

Step 5: Creating a Group for Categorizing Products

1. To create a group for categorizing products by profitability, follow these steps:

  - In the "Data" pane on the left, right-click on the "Profit" field.

  - Select "Create" and then choose "Group."

  - In the "Create Group" dialog, define your group categories. For example, you can create categories like "High Profit," "Medium Profit," and "Low Profit."

  - Name your group, e.g., "Profit Categories."

2. Tableau will create a new dimension that represents your grouped categories.

Step 6: Categorizing Products by Profitability

1. To categorize products by profitability, drag the "Profit Categories" group to the Rows shelf before the "Product Name" field.

2. This will create a grouped view where products are categorized by their profitability.

Step 7: Customizing and Formatting

1. You can customize your visualization by adjusting colors, labels, and formatting to make the set and group visualizations more informative.

Step 8: Review and Output Data

1. Review your set and group visualizations to ensure they meet your analysis objectives.

2. Output your results in Tableau worksheets, dashboards, or reports for presentation or exploration.

Step 9: Advanced Set and Group Options

1. Tableau offers advanced options for sets and groups, such as combined fields, calculated sets, and dynamic groups based on conditions.

2. You can create calculated sets and groups that adapt to changing data conditions.

Step 10: Review and Adjust Sets and Groups

1. Regularly review and adjust your sets and groups as your analysis evolves.

2. Modify conditions for sets and refine group categories as needed.

By following these steps and utilizing Tableau's sets and groups, you can create custom subsets of data and categorize information for more effective analysis. Whether you're highlighting top-performing data points or categorizing data into meaningful groups, Tableau provides the flexibility and tools to organize and analyze your data efficiently.

In summary, sets and groups are powerful features in Tableau that enable you to create custom subsets and categorize data for more effective analysis. Sets help you highlight specific data points, while groups allow you to structure your data for meaningful insights. These features are particularly valuable when you need to categorize data by specific criteria or highlight specific data points based on conditions.

Advanced data blending techniques

Data blending is a critical process in Tableau that allows you to combine data from multiple sources to create comprehensive visualizations and analyses. In this section, we will explore advanced data blending techniques using Tableau.

Example: Combining Data from Multiple Sources

Scenario: You have sales data in one database and customer data in another, and you want to combine these datasets to analyze sales by customer segment. We'll use advanced data blending techniques to accomplish this.

Step 1: Connect to Data Sources

1. Open Tableau and create a new workbook.

2. Connect to the sales data source (e.g., a database containing sales information).

3. Connect to the customer data source (e.g., a database containing customer information).

Step 2: Data Source Configuration

1. In the Data Source tab, make sure to properly configure the connections for both data sources. Ensure that the common field(s) for blending are recognized and match between the sources.

2. Define the relationship between the data sources by joining them on the common field(s).

Step 3: Creating Blended Data Source

1. In the Data Source tab, you can see both data sources listed. Drag the required fields from each data source into the Data Source tab to create a blended data source.

2. Use the blending icon (a linking chain) to define how the data is linked between the two sources.

Step 4: Building Visualizations

1. Create a new worksheet in Tableau.

2. Drag the "Sales" field from the blended data source to the Columns shelf.

3. Drag the "Customer Segment" field from the blended data source to the Rows shelf.

4. You can now create various visualizations such as bar charts, line charts, or tables to analyze sales by customer segment.

Step 5: Customizing and Formatting

1. Customize your visualizations with appropriate colors, labels, and formatting options.

2. Add titles and descriptions to make the insights more understandable.

Step 6: Filters and Parameters

1. Apply filters and parameters to allow users to interact with the visualizations and explore the data more effectively.

2. Create dynamic filters or parameters for different aspects of the analysis.

Step 7: Aggregations and Calculations

1. Use aggregations and calculations to perform advanced analysis on the blended data.

2. Calculate metrics such as profit margins, growth rates, or customer retention.

Step 8: Dashboard Creation

1. You can create dashboards to bring multiple visualizations together.

2. Dashboards allow you to present a holistic view of your blended data and provide a more interactive experience.

Step 9: Publishing and Sharing

1. Once you've built your analysis, you can publish it to Tableau Server or Tableau Online to share it with your team or stakeholders.

2. Set permissions and access controls to ensure the right people can view and interact with your data.

Step 10: Ongoing Data Blending

1. Data sources may change over time, so it's essential to maintain and update your data blending configurations as needed.

2. Be prepared to adapt to evolving data sources and requirements.

In summary, advanced data blending in Tableau allows you to combine data from different sources to create meaningful insights and visualizations. By configuring the relationships between data sources, blending fields, and building customized visualizations, you can gain a comprehensive understanding of your data. Whether you're analyzing sales by customer segments or merging data from multiple databases, Tableau's advanced data blending techniques provide a powerful toolset for data analysts and business professionals.

Combining data from different file types

Data often comes in various formats and file types. Tableau offers the flexibility to blend and combine data from different file types to create comprehensive visualizations and analyses. In this section, we will explore how to combine data from different file types in Tableau.

Example: Blending CSV and Excel Files

Scenario: You have sales data in a CSV file and customer data in an Excel spreadsheet, and you want to blend these datasets to analyze sales by customer segment. We'll use Tableau to perform this data blending.

Step 1: Connect to Data Sources

1. Open Tableau and create a new workbook.

2. Connect to the CSV file containing your sales data.

3. Connect to the Excel file containing your customer data.

Step 2: Data Source Configuration

1. In the Data Source tab, ensure that both data sources are properly configured. Define the common field(s) for blending.

2. If necessary, adjust the data source configurations, such as identifying header rows or specifying data types.

Step 3: Creating Blended Data Source

1. In the Data Source tab, you can see both data sources listed. Drag the required fields from each data source into the Data Source tab to create a blended data source.

2. Use the blending icon (a linking chain) to define how the data is linked between the two sources.

Step 4: Building Visualizations

1. Create a new worksheet in Tableau.

2. Drag the "Sales" field from the blended data source to the Columns shelf.

3. Drag the "Customer Segment" field from the blended data source to the Rows shelf.

4. Create visualizations such as bar charts, line charts, or tables to analyze sales by customer segment.

Step 5: Customizing and Formatting

1. Customize your visualizations with appropriate colors, labels, and formatting options.

2. Add titles and descriptions to make the insights more understandable.

Step 6: Filters and Parameters

1. Apply filters and parameters to allow users to interact with the visualizations and explore the data more effectively.

2. Create dynamic filters or parameters for different aspects of the analysis.

Step 7: Aggregations and Calculations

1. Use aggregations and calculations to perform advanced analysis on the blended data.

2. Calculate metrics such as profit margins, growth rates, or customer retention.

Step 8: Dashboard Creation

1. You can create dashboards to bring multiple visualizations together.

2. Dashboards allow you to present a holistic view of your blended data and provide a more interactive experience.

Step 9: Publishing and Sharing

1. Once you've built your analysis, you can publish it to Tableau Server or Tableau Online to share it with your team or stakeholders.

2. Set permissions and access controls to ensure the right people can view and interact with your data.

Step 10: Ongoing Data Blending

1. Data sources may change over time, so it's essential to maintain and update your data blending configurations as needed.

2. Be prepared to adapt to evolving data sources and requirements.

In summary, Tableau enables you to seamlessly blend data from different file types and formats, such as CSV and Excel files. By configuring the relationships between data sources, blending fields, and building customized visualizations, you can gain a comprehensive understanding of your data. Whether you're analyzing sales by customer segments or merging data from various file types, Tableau's advanced data blending capabilities provide a powerful toolset for data analysts and business professionals.

Data mashups for enriched analysis

Data mashups involve combining data from multiple sources, which can include databases, web services, APIs, and other sources, to create a richer dataset for analysis. In this section, we'll explore how to perform data mashups in Tableau for enriched analysis.

Example: Mashing Up Sales Data and Weather Data

Scenario: You have sales data and weather data from different sources, and you want to analyze how weather conditions affect your sales performance. We'll use Tableau to perform a data mashup to achieve this.

Step 1: Connect to Data Sources

1. Open Tableau and create a new workbook.

2. Connect to the sales data source, which may be a database or a CSV file.

3. Connect to the weather data source, which can be retrieved from a web service or an API.

Step 2: Data Source Configuration

1. Ensure that both data sources are correctly configured and that you've identified the common field(s) for data blending.

2. If necessary, specify data types, date formats, and any other data source configurations.

Step 3: Creating a Blended Data Source

1. In the Data Source tab, you'll see both data sources listed. Drag the required fields from each source into the Data Source tab to create a blended data source.

2. Use the blending icon (a linking chain) to specify how the data is linked between the two sources, which may involve date-based matching or other criteria.

Step 4: Building Visualizations

1. Create a new worksheet in Tableau.

2. Drag the "Sales" field from the blended data source to the Columns shelf.

3. Drag relevant weather-related fields from the blended data source to the Rows shelf.

4. Create visualizations that help analyze the relationship between weather conditions and sales, such as line charts or scatter plots.

Step 5: Customizing and Formatting

1. Customize your visualizations with suitable colors, labels, and formatting options.

2. Add titles, descriptions, and annotations to highlight key insights related to the mashup.

Step 6: Filters and Parameters

1. Apply filters and parameters to allow users to interact with the visualizations and explore the data more effectively.

2. Consider creating dynamic filters that let users adjust date ranges, weather conditions, or other factors affecting the analysis.

Step 7: Aggregations and Calculations

1. Use aggregations and calculations to perform advanced analysis on the mashed-up data. For instance, calculate correlations between sales and weather variables.

2. Explore the use of calculated fields to derive additional insights.

Step 8: Dashboard Creation

1. Build a dashboard that combines multiple visualizations and provides an overview of the mashed-up data.

2. Dashboards allow you to present a holistic view of your analysis, incorporating different aspects of the mashup.

Step 9: Publishing and Sharing

1. After completing your analysis, publish it to Tableau Server or Tableau Online to share it with relevant stakeholders.

2. Set permissions and access controls to ensure that the right individuals can access and interact with your enriched analysis.

Step 10: Ongoing Data Mashups

1. Data sources and requirements can evolve. Be prepared to update and refine your data mashup configurations as needed.

2. Continuous monitoring of data sources and their quality is crucial to maintaining the accuracy of your enriched analysis.

In summary, Tableau empowers you to perform data mashups to enrich your analysis by combining data from various sources, such as sales and weather data. By configuring the relationships between data sources, blending fields, and creating customized visualizations, you can gain valuable insights into how external factors influence your data. Data mashups are a powerful tool for data analysts and business professionals seeking a deeper understanding of their data and its real-world context.

Handling data discrepancies and inconsistencies

In the world of data blending and mashups, it's common to encounter data discrepancies and inconsistencies between different sources. These can include variations in data formats, missing data, or differences in data granularity. In this section, we'll discuss strategies for handling these challenges.

Example: Merging Sales Data from Multiple Locations

Scenario: You have sales data from multiple store locations, and each location's data is stored in different formats and structures. We'll use Tableau to merge this data while addressing discrepancies and inconsistencies.

Step 1: Data Assessment and Profiling

1. Begin by thoroughly understanding the structure and format of the data from each location. This includes identifying data types, column names, and any potential variations.

2. Use Tableau's data profiling features to get a detailed overview of the data, including data quality, missing values, and data distributions.

Step 2: Data Cleaning and Transformation

1. Standardize the data by renaming columns and ensuring consistent data types. For example, if one location records "January" as "Jan," while another uses "01," standardize it to a common format.

2. Deal with missing data by filling in gaps or using data imputation techniques, such as using the average of nearby data points.

3. If the data is at different granularities (e.g., daily sales for one location and hourly sales for another), consider aggregating the higher granularity data or expanding the lower granularity data to match.

Step 3: Data Blending in Tableau

1. In Tableau, connect to the cleaned and transformed data from each location.

2. Use Tableau's data blending feature to bring the data sources together. Identify a common field or set of fields to link the data sources.

3. Define relationships between the data sources, considering the blending keys, filters, and hierarchies.

Step 4: Data Blending Challenges

1. During the blending process, you may encounter issues like data duplication, null values, or unexpected join results. Utilize Tableau's troubleshooting tools to identify and resolve these challenges.

2. Consider using calculated fields to handle specific data transformation requirements during the blending process.

Step 5: Data Quality Assessment

1. After blending the data, perform a quality assessment to ensure the merged dataset is accurate and coherent.

2. Check for discrepancies in aggregated results, and validate the data consistency across locations.

Step 6: Visualization and Analysis

1. Build visualizations and analyses to explore the combined data. Use Tableau's features to filter, sort, and group the data to gain insights.

2. Create calculated fields if needed to perform analyses that span the merged data.

Step 7: Documentation and Validation

1. Document the data blending process, any transformation steps, and any calculated fields created during the merging process.

2. Validate the results with stakeholders to ensure that the merged data aligns with business requirements.

Step 8: Ongoing Data Governance

1. Establish data governance practices to maintain data consistency and quality as new data is added to the merged dataset.

2. Ensure that the process can be scaled and automated to handle future data from different locations.

In summary, handling data discrepancies and inconsistencies during advanced data blending and mashup processes is a critical aspect of data preparation. By assessing, cleaning, and transforming data from various sources and using Tableau's data blending capabilities, you can create a comprehensive dataset for analysis while addressing the challenges that arise from differences in data structure and quality. This process enables more accurate and insightful analysis, making it a valuable skill for data professionals and analysts.

CHAPTER V
Advanced Analysis Techniques

5.1 Statistical Analysis with Tableau

Introduction to statistical functions in Tableau

Tableau offers a range of powerful statistical functions that allow you to perform in-depth statistical analysis on your data. In this section, we'll introduce you to these functions, explain their applications, and provide step-by-step guidance on how to use them effectively.

Example: Performing Statistical Analysis on Sales Data

Scenario: You have a dataset containing sales data for a retail company and want to perform statistical analysis to gain insights into sales trends.

Step 1: Understanding Statistical Functions

Before we dive into the specific functions, let's understand what Tableau's statistical functions can do:

- **Percentile:** Calculates percentiles for a specified measure, helping you understand data distribution.

- **Correlation:** Measures the strength and direction of a linear relationship between two variables.

- **Covariance:** Quantifies the degree to which two variables change together.

- **Z-Score:** Calculates the number of standard deviations a data point is from the mean, helping identify outliers.

- **T-Test:** Performs hypothesis testing to compare means between two groups.

- **ANOVA:** Analyzes variance between groups to determine if there are statistically significant differences.

Step 2: Data Preparation

Ensure your data is clean and organized. It should contain the variables you want to perform statistical analysis on.

Step 3: Creating Calculated Fields

1. In Tableau, open the calculated field editor.

2. Select the statistical function you want to use (e.g., Percentile, Correlation).

3. Define the function parameters. For example, when calculating the correlation between sales and advertising spending, you'd select these two measures.

4. The calculated field generates the desired statistical result.

Step 4: Visualizing Results

1. Create visualizations that use the calculated fields. For example, you can create a scatter plot to visualize the correlation between two variables.

Step 5: Interpreting Results

Understand the meaning and implications of the statistical analysis:

- For correlation and covariance, values close to 1 indicate a strong positive relationship, while values close to -1 indicate a strong negative relationship.

- For percentiles, you can analyze data distribution by comparing data points with percentiles.

- For t-tests and ANOVA, consider p-values. Lower p-values indicate stronger evidence against the null hypothesis.

Step 6: Revising and Iterating

Use the insights gained from statistical analysis to make data-driven decisions. If needed, revise your analysis by adjusting parameters or exploring different statistical functions.

Step 7: Documentation and Communication

Document your statistical analysis process, including the functions used and their results. Clearly communicate your findings to stakeholders.

Best Practices for Statistical Analysis in Tableau

1. Understand your data: Thoroughly grasp the characteristics and context of your data before applying statistical functions.

2. Choose the right statistical function: Select the function that best matches your analytical goals.

3. Visualize results: Create visualizations to make your statistical findings more accessible and actionable.

4. Validate your results: If you obtain significant findings, perform hypothesis testing to ensure the results are statistically sound.

5. Use statistical analysis responsibly: Keep ethical and privacy considerations in mind when analyzing data, especially when working with sensitive information.

In summary, Tableau's statistical functions provide a powerful toolkit for data analysts and scientists to gain deeper insights from their data. By following the steps outlined in this section and adhering to best practices, you can harness the full potential of these functions to make informed decisions and drive business success.

Descriptive statistics and distribution analysis

Statistical analysis in Tableau can provide valuable insights into your data's characteristics and distribution. In this section, we'll explore how to perform descriptive statistics and distribution analysis using Tableau.

Scenario: Analyzing Sales Data

Scenario: You have a dataset containing monthly sales data for a retail company and want to perform descriptive statistics and distribution analysis to understand the sales trends.

Step 1: Data Preparation

Ensure your data is clean, well-organized, and contains the variables you want to analyze. In this case, you'll need the "Month" and "Sales" columns.

Step 2: Descriptive Statistics

Tableau offers a range of descriptive statistics functions, such as mean, median, mode, standard deviation, and quartiles. Here's how to use them:

1. Create a calculated field in Tableau.

2. Select the desired descriptive statistic function (e.g., `SUM`, `AVG`, `MEDIAN`, `STDEV`).

3. Apply the function to the "Sales" column.

4. The calculated field will display the descriptive statistic for your sales data.

Step 3: Distribution Analysis

Understanding data distribution is crucial. Tableau provides various visualizations for distribution analysis:

1. Histogram: Create a histogram to visualize the frequency distribution of sales values. You can do this by creating a histogram chart in Tableau with "Sales" on the x-axis and "Count of Records" on the y-axis.

2. Box Plot: Box plots are useful for understanding data dispersion and identifying outliers. Create a box plot with "Sales" as the measure and "Month" as the dimension.

Step 4: Visualizing the Analysis

1. Use the calculated fields and distribution visualizations in your worksheets or dashboards.

2. For descriptive statistics, consider displaying the values as text on a dashboard or worksheet.

3. For distribution analysis, create a visualization with your histogram or box plot.

Step 5: Interpreting Results

- Descriptive statistics help you understand central tendencies (mean, median) and dispersion (standard deviation) of your sales data.

- For distribution analysis, check the shape and spread of the histogram and look for any outliers in the box plot.

Step 6: Iterating and Insights

Use the insights gained from your analysis to make data-driven decisions. If you find unexpected results or outliers, consider conducting further investigations or hypothesis testing.

Step 7: Documentation and Communication

Document your descriptive statistics and distribution analysis findings. Clearly communicate your results to stakeholders using visuals and explanations.

Best Practices for Descriptive Statistics and Distribution Analysis

1. Choose the right descriptive statistics: Select the most relevant descriptive statistics functions based on your analysis goals.

2. Visualize distributions effectively: Use appropriate visualizations, such as histograms and box plots, to represent your data's distribution.

3. Understand the context: Interpret your analysis in the context of your business or research objectives.

4. Validate your findings: Ensure your analysis is statistically sound, and consider further testing if necessary.

5. Keep data privacy in mind: Be cautious when dealing with sensitive information, especially when sharing results.

In summary, Tableau provides a powerful platform for conducting descriptive statistics and distribution analysis, enabling you to uncover valuable insights from your data. By following the steps and best practices outlined in this section, you can harness the full potential of Tableau for informed decision-making.

Hypothesis testing and statistical significance

Hypothesis testing is a critical component of statistical analysis that allows us to draw conclusions about data. In this section, we will explore how to perform hypothesis testing using Tableau and evaluate the statistical significance of your findings.

Scenario: Analyzing A/B Test Results

Scenario: You work for an e-commerce company that recently conducted an A/B test to determine whether a new website design (Version B) leads to higher conversion rates compared to the old design (Version A). You have data on user interactions with both versions and want to test the hypothesis.

Step 1: Formulate Hypotheses

In hypothesis testing, you typically have two hypotheses:

- Null Hypothesis (H0): This hypothesis suggests that any observed differences are due to chance. In our scenario, H0 might state that there is no significant difference in conversion rates between Version A and Version B.

- Alternative Hypothesis (H1 or Ha): This hypothesis suggests that there is a significant difference. In our scenario, Ha would state that Version B leads to higher conversion rates than Version A.

Step 2: Data Preparation

Ensure your data is clean, well-organized, and contains the variables needed for your A/B test analysis, such as user interactions and the version each user was exposed to.

Step 3: Perform the Test

In Tableau, you can use calculated fields and visualizations to perform a hypothesis test:

1. Calculate the conversion rate for each version using a calculated field. For example, "Conversion Rate = SUM([Converted]) / COUNTD([User ID])."

2. Create a visualization to compare the conversion rates of Version A and Version B. You can use a bar chart or other suitable visualizations.

3. Use the built-in Tableau functionality to perform a two-sample t-test (assuming your data meets the assumptions of this test). You can do this by right-clicking on the visualization and selecting "Test Hypotheses."

Step 4: Interpret the Results

The output of your hypothesis test will provide a p-value. A low p-value (typically below 0.05) indicates that you can reject the null hypothesis in favor of the alternative hypothesis, suggesting that there is a significant difference.

Step 5: Visualize the Findings

Create visualizations that communicate the results of your hypothesis test. You can use a summary visualization, highlighting the significant difference in conversion rates.

Step 6: Report and Communicate

Clearly document your findings, including the p-value and whether you rejected the null hypothesis. Share the results with stakeholders and provide actionable insights based on your findings.

Best Practices for Hypothesis Testing with Tableau

1. Carefully define your hypotheses: Make sure your null and alternative hypotheses are clear and specific to your research question.

2. Ensure data quality: Clean and prepare your data to ensure accurate results.

3. Understand assumptions: Be aware of the assumptions of the statistical test you choose and check if they hold for your data.

4. Visualize results: Create compelling visualizations that make it easy for stakeholders to understand your findings.

5. Provide context: Explain the practical significance of your results and their implications for the business.

In summary, Tableau can be a valuable tool for performing hypothesis testing and assessing the statistical significance of your findings. By following the steps and best practices outlined in this section, you can effectively analyze A/B test results and make data-informed decisions for your organization.

Regression analysis and predictive modeling

Regression analysis and predictive modeling are powerful tools for understanding relationships between variables and making predictions based on data. In this section, we will explore how to perform regression analysis and predictive modeling using Tableau.

Scenario: Sales Prediction for an E-commerce Store

Scenario: You are a data analyst for an e-commerce store, and your goal is to predict future sales based on historical data. You have access to data that includes variables like advertising spend, website traffic, and past sales figures.

Step 1: Data Preparation

Ensure your data is clean, organized, and contains the relevant variables, such as sales, advertising spend, and website traffic. Tableau requires structured data for regression analysis.

Step 2: Create a Scatter Plot

1. In Tableau, create a scatter plot with sales on the y-axis and the predictor variable (e.g., advertising spend) on the x-axis. This helps visualize the relationship between variables.

2. Add a trend line to the scatter plot. The trend line will show the linear relationship between the variables.

Step 3: Perform Linear Regression

1. Right-click the trend line on the scatter plot and select "Describe." Tableau will provide a summary of the linear relationship and the R-squared value, which measures the goodness of fit.

2. You can also perform multiple linear regression by adding multiple predictor variables. Create a calculated field to combine variables, if necessary.

Step 4: Create a Predictive Model

1. In Tableau, you can use predictive modeling to make future sales predictions. Create a calculated field using a linear regression model, including predictor variables and coefficients.

2. Visualize your predictive model by adding it to a chart. You can create a time series chart to see predicted sales over time.

Step 5: Evaluate and Validate

1. Evaluate the performance of your predictive model using metrics such as Mean Absolute Error (MAE) or Mean Squared Error (MSE).

2. Split your data into training and testing sets to validate the accuracy of your model. Use Tableau's features to split and assess your model's performance.

Step 6: Apply Predictions

Use the predictive model to make sales predictions for future periods. You can add these predictions to your dashboard to track forecasted sales alongside historical data.

Best Practices for Regression Analysis and Predictive Modeling with Tableau

1. Choose appropriate variables: Select predictor variables that are logically related to the outcome you want to predict.

2. Visualize relationships: Scatter plots and trend lines provide an initial understanding of relationships between variables.

3. Interpret coefficients: Understand the meaning of coefficients in regression models. Positive coefficients indicate a positive relationship, while negative coefficients suggest a negative relationship.

4. Evaluate model performance: Use relevant metrics to assess how well your predictive model performs.

5. Communicate results: Clearly present your findings and predictions in a visually compelling way using Tableau dashboards.

In summary, Tableau can be a valuable tool for regression analysis and predictive modeling. By following the steps and best practices outlined in this section, you can effectively analyze data and make data-driven predictions for your organization.

5.2 Trend and Forecast Analysis

Identifying trends in data using trend lines

Trend analysis is a fundamental part of data analysis, allowing you to uncover patterns, make forecasts, and gain insights into your data. Tableau provides tools to identify trends and make forecasts based on historical data. In this section, we will explore how to identify trends in your data using trend lines in Tableau.

Step 1: Data Preparation

Before you begin, ensure that your data is well-structured and contains a time-related field, such as date or time. Trend analysis is particularly useful when dealing with time series data.

Step 2: Create a Line Chart

1. In Tableau, start by creating a line chart. Place the time-related field (e.g., the date) on the x-axis and the variable you want to analyze (e.g., sales, stock prices) on the y-axis.

2. You can also add more dimensions to the view to analyze trends across different categories or dimensions.

Step 3: Add a Trend Line

1. After creating the line chart, right-click on the chart, and select "Add Trend Line."

2. You can choose from different trend line types, such as linear, exponential, logarithmic, polynomial, or moving average. The appropriate trend line type depends on your data and the type of trend you want to analyze.

Step 4: Analyze the Trend Line

1. Interpret the trend line's slope and direction. A positive slope indicates an upward trend, while a negative slope indicates a downward trend.

2. Pay attention to the R-squared value provided by Tableau. This value measures the goodness of fit of the trend line. A higher R-squared value indicates a better fit.

Step 5: Create Forecasts

1. To make forecasts, right-click on the trend line and select "Describe."

2. In the trend line description, you'll find options for forecasting. Specify the number of periods you want to forecast into the future.

3. Tableau will automatically generate a forecast that extends beyond your data points. The forecast is represented by a dashed line on the chart.

Step 6: Customize the Trend Analysis

1. Customize your trend analysis by adjusting the forecast options, trend line options, and other settings available in Tableau.

2. You can add reference lines, annotations, and other visual elements to enhance your trend analysis.

Best Practices for Trend Analysis in Tableau

1. Understand your data: Before performing trend analysis, have a clear understanding of the data and the problem you're trying to address.

2. Choose the right trend line type: Select the appropriate trend line type based on the characteristics of your data. Different trends may require different line types.

3. Use filters: Apply filters to focus on specific time periods or data subsets to get a more detailed view of trends.

4. Compare trends: Create multiple trend lines to compare different metrics or dimensions within the same chart.

5. Be cautious with long-term forecasts: While forecasting is valuable, long-term forecasts can be less accurate. Use forecasts as a guide rather than absolute predictions.

Trend analysis in Tableau allows you to uncover valuable insights, make data-driven decisions, and communicate trends effectively to your audience. By following the steps and best practices in this section, you can harness the power of trend analysis in your data analysis projects.

Time series analysis and forecasting

Time series analysis and forecasting are powerful techniques to understand and predict trends in data over a specific period. Whether you're dealing with sales figures, stock prices, or any other time-dependent data, Tableau can help you perform time series analysis and make forecasts. In this section, we will explore how to conduct time series analysis and forecasting using Tableau.

Step 1: Data Preparation

Before starting, ensure your data is in a time-series format, with a clear date or time field and the variable of interest you want to analyze.

Step 2: Create a Time Series Plot

1. Open Tableau and connect to your dataset.

2. Drag the date or time field to the Columns shelf to create a time series chart.

3. Drag the variable you want to analyze to the Rows shelf.

Step 3: Adding Time Periods

1. Tableau often provides options for aggregating time periods. For instance, you can choose to visualize data by days, months, quarters, or years. Right-click on the date field and choose your preferred time period.

Step 4: Analyzing Trends

1. With the time series chart, you can visually inspect trends, seasonality, and any irregular patterns in your data.

2. To analyze trends, right-click on the chart, select "Trend Lines," and choose the type of trend line that best fits your data.

3. The trend line helps you understand whether your data exhibits an upward, downward, or flat trend.

Step 5: Making Forecasts

1. To make forecasts, right-click on the trend line, and select "Describe."

2. In the forecasting options, specify the number of periods into the future you want to forecast.

3. Tableau will automatically generate a forecast for the selected variable. The forecasted data is represented with dashed lines on the chart.

Step 6: Customizing Forecast Settings

1. Tableau provides several customization options for forecasts. You can adjust forecast options and confidence intervals to fine-tune your predictions.

Step 7: Evaluate Forecast Accuracy

1. Evaluate the accuracy of your forecast by checking the forecasted data against actual data. A good practice is to compare your forecast to historical data to assess the model's reliability.

Step 8: Exploring Seasonal Decomposition

1. Seasonal decomposition helps break down the time series data into its trend, seasonality, and residual components. Right-click on the chart and choose "Decompose."

2. This decomposition is beneficial for understanding the cyclic patterns and the impact of seasonality in your data.

Best Practices for Time Series Analysis and Forecasting

1. Understand your data: Gain a deep understanding of the underlying patterns, seasonality, and any anomalies in your time series data.

2. Test different time periods: Experiment with different time aggregation levels to gain insights into your data from various perspectives.

3. Validate your model: Validate the accuracy of your forecasts by comparing them with actual data and by using metrics like Mean Absolute Error (MAE) and Root Mean Squared Error (RMSE).

4. Seasonal decomposition: Decompose your time series to understand the individual effects of trend, seasonality, and residual components.

5. Use confidence intervals: Leverage confidence intervals in your forecasts to assess the uncertainty of future predictions.

Time series analysis and forecasting in Tableau allow you to make informed decisions and predictions based on historical data. By following the steps and best practices in this section, you can effectively conduct time series analysis and make accurate forecasts.

Creating moving averages and exponential smoothing

In this section, we'll explore the use of moving averages and exponential smoothing for time series data analysis in Tableau. These techniques are valuable for understanding and forecasting trends within your data.

Moving Averages:

Moving averages are a widely used technique to smooth out variations in time series data and identify trends. They are calculated by averaging a specific number of data points within a moving window. Here's how to create moving averages in Tableau:

Step 1: Data Preparation:

Ensure your data is in a time series format and is connected to Tableau.

Step 2: Creating a Moving Average:

1. Open Tableau and connect to your dataset.

2. Drag the date or time field to the Columns shelf.

3. Drag the variable you want to analyze to the Rows shelf.

4. Right-click on the variable in the Rows shelf, and select "Create" > "Moving Calculation."

5. In the dialog that appears, you can configure the type of calculation you want (e.g., simple moving average, weighted moving average), the number of periods to include in the average, and more.

6. Click "OK" to create the moving average.

7. The moving average will appear on your chart, smoothing out the data and making trends more apparent.

Exponential Smoothing:

Exponential smoothing is another technique used for forecasting and trend analysis. It gives more weight to recent data points, making it suitable for capturing rapid changes in data. Here's how to create exponential smoothing in Tableau:

Step 1: Data Preparation:

Ensure your data is in a time series format and is connected to Tableau.

Step 2: Creating Exponential Smoothing:

1. Follow the same steps as for creating a moving average.

2. Right-click on the variable in the Rows shelf, and select "Create" > "Exponential Smoothing."

3. In the dialog that appears, you can configure the level of smoothing (alpha parameter), which determines the weight given to recent data. Lower alpha values give more weight to older data, while higher alpha values emphasize recent data.

4. Click "OK" to create the exponential smoothing.

5. The exponential smoothing line will appear on your chart, providing a smoothed representation of your data.

Choosing the Right Technique:

The choice between moving averages and exponential smoothing depends on your specific data and the nature of the trends you want to capture. Moving averages are suitable for capturing longer-term trends, while exponential smoothing is better at capturing rapid changes and short-term trends.

Best Practices for Moving Averages and Exponential Smoothing:

1. Experiment with different time windows and smoothing parameters to find the best fit for your data.

2. Validate the accuracy of your smoothed data by comparing it to actual data and using relevant metrics.

By utilizing moving averages and exponential smoothing in Tableau, you can gain insights into the trends within your time series data and make more accurate forecasts. These techniques are invaluable for business intelligence, financial analysis, and various other applications.

Visualizing forecasts and trend predictions

In this section, we will delve into visualizing forecasts and trend predictions in Tableau. After performing trend and forecast analysis on your data, it's crucial to present the results in an understandable and compelling manner.

Visualizing Forecasts:

Once you have generated forecasts and predictions using techniques like moving averages or exponential smoothing, you can create visualizations to represent these predictions effectively. Here's how to do it:

Step 1: Data and Forecast Preparation:

Ensure that you have performed trend and forecast analysis on your data and that your dataset includes both historical data and forecasted values.

Step 2: Creating Visualizations:

1. Open Tableau and connect to your dataset.

2. Drag the date or time field to the Columns shelf.

3. Drag the variable you've forecasted (e.g., sales, revenue) to the Rows shelf.

4. To visualize the historical data, select the appropriate chart type, such as a line chart or an area chart. Drag the date field to the "Color" shelf to distinguish between historical and forecasted data.

5. To add the forecasted values, you can follow these steps:

a. Create a calculated field for your forecasted variable. For example, if you've generated a moving average forecast, create a calculated field that combines historical data and forecasted values.

b. Drag this calculated field to the Rows shelf to overlay the forecast on the historical data.

c. You can format the forecasted data points differently, for example, by changing the shape or color of the data points to distinguish them from the historical data.

6. Add labels or annotations to the chart to provide context and explain the forecasted values to your audience.

Choosing the Right Visualization:

The choice of visualization depends on your data and the type of forecast you've generated. Line charts, area charts, or combination charts can effectively display historical data and forecasts. Additionally, you can use reference lines to highlight specific forecasted values or trends.

Visualizing Trends:

To visualize trends identified in your data, you can use various charts and techniques. Some options include:

1. Trend Lines: Add trend lines to your line or scatter plots to make trends more apparent. Right-click on a chart, select "Trend Lines," and choose the type of line (e.g., linear, exponential, moving average) that best represents the trend.

2. Heat Maps: Use heat maps to display trends or patterns over time. Color-coding can help users quickly identify trends or changes in your data.

3. Area Charts: Area charts are useful for showing cumulative data or how one variable contributes to a total over time.

Best Practices for Visualizing Forecasts and Trends:

1. Keep your visualizations clear and straightforward. Avoid clutter and overcomplicated charts that may confuse the audience.

2. Use annotations, labels, and tooltips to provide additional information and context for your visualizations.

3. Ensure that your visualizations are appropriately labeled, with clear titles and axis labels.

4. Consider the audience's level of data literacy and tailor your visualizations accordingly.

Visualizing forecasts and trends is essential for conveying the insights gained from your data analysis effectively. With Tableau's powerful visualization capabilities, you can create compelling and informative charts that help stakeholders understand the patterns and predictions within your data.

5.3 What-If Analysis and Scenario Planning

What-if parameters and scenario analysis

What-If Analysis is a powerful feature in Tableau that allows you to explore different scenarios and understand how changes to specific parameters or variables can affect your data and, consequently, your business outcomes. In this section, we will explore how to perform What-If Analysis using parameters and conduct scenario planning in Tableau.

Step 1: Creating a What-If Parameter:

1. Open Tableau and connect to your dataset.

2. Identify the variable you want to explore in your What-If Analysis. For example, you might want to analyze the impact of changes in the discount rate on sales.

3. Right-click on a blank space in the Data pane and select "Create Parameter."

4. Define the parameter:

   - Name: Give it a descriptive name (e.g., Discount Rate).

   - Data Type: Choose the appropriate data type (usually float or integer).

   - Allowable Values: Choose "All" to allow any value within the defined range.

   - Range: Define the minimum and maximum values based on the variable you are analyzing (e.g., 0 to 1 for a discount rate).

5. Create a calculated field that uses the What-If Parameter. For instance, if you're exploring the impact of the discount rate on sales, you can create a calculated field that multiplies the discount rate parameter by the sales variable.

Step 2: Using the What-If Parameter:

1. Drag the calculated field that uses the What-If Parameter to your visualization. This can be a line chart, bar chart, or any other chart type that suits your analysis.

2. Create a control for the parameter by right-clicking on the parameter in the Data pane and selecting "Show Parameter Control." This adds a slider or input box to your worksheet.

Step 3: Exploring Scenarios:

With the parameter control in place, you can now easily explore different scenarios:

1. Adjust the parameter using the slider or input box. For example, change the discount rate from 0.1 to 0.2.

2. Observe how the chart updates in real-time to reflect the new parameter value. You can see how changes in the discount rate impact the visualized data.

3. You can create multiple calculated fields and parameter controls for different variables to perform more complex What-If Analysis. For instance, you can explore the combined impact of changes in both discount rate and advertising spend on sales.

Scenario Planning:

Scenario planning involves creating multiple What-If Parameters and conducting analysis for a range of scenarios. This can help you make informed decisions based on the possible outcomes of various scenarios.

1. Create additional What-If Parameters for different variables you want to analyze.

2. Set up a dashboard that includes multiple parameter controls for these parameters.

3. As you adjust the parameters to simulate different scenarios, you can visualize how each scenario affects your data and make informed business decisions accordingly.

Best Practices:

- Keep your parameter names and descriptions clear and intuitive.

- Ensure that the parameter range covers a realistic and relevant span of values.

- Use tooltips and annotations to provide context and explanations in your visualizations.

- Combine What-If Analysis with other Tableau features like dashboards and actions for a more interactive and comprehensive analysis.

What-If Analysis and scenario planning in Tableau provide valuable insights for decision-makers by allowing them to explore the potential impact of different variables on their data. By creating and adjusting parameters, you can simulate a wide range of scenarios, enabling more informed and strategic decision-making.

Scenario planning and sensitivity analysis

Scenario planning is a crucial element of What-If Analysis that helps you explore various possible future scenarios by changing multiple variables simultaneously and understanding the potential impact of these changes on your data. Sensitivity analysis, on the other hand, is a quantitative method used to determine how sensitive a particular outcome is to variations in input variables. In this section, we will delve into scenario planning and sensitivity analysis using Tableau.

Step 1: Defining Scenarios for Scenario Planning:

1. Open Tableau and load your dataset.

2. Identify the variables that you want to explore in your scenario planning. For example, you may want to understand how variations in advertising spend, product prices, and discount rates affect your sales.

3. Create What-If Parameters for each variable of interest, following the steps outlined in the previous section.

Step 2: Building Scenarios:

1. In Tableau, create a calculated field for each scenario you want to analyze. This calculated field should use the What-If Parameters to adjust the variables of interest. For instance, if you're analyzing the effect of advertising spend, you can create a calculated field that multiplies the original advertising spend by your What-If Parameter.

2. Develop different calculated fields for each scenario you want to consider. Let's say you're interested in low, base, and high scenarios for advertising spend, discount rates, and product prices. Create a calculated field for each combination (e.g., low advertising spend, high discount rate, and low product prices).

Step 3: Visualizing Scenarios:

1. Create a visualization (e.g., a line chart) and add your calculated fields (scenarios) to the Columns or Rows shelf, depending on the type of chart.

2. Use your parameter controls for each What-If Parameter to switch between scenarios. As you adjust these parameters, you can instantly see how they impact your data, allowing you to compare scenarios easily.

Step 4: Analyzing Sensitivity:

1. Sensitivity analysis helps you understand the sensitivity of your key performance indicators (KPIs) to changes in various input variables. You can create sensitivity scenarios by incrementally varying a single input variable and observing the changes in your KPIs.

2. Create calculated fields that represent the incremental changes in input variables (e.g., a 10% increase or decrease in advertising spend) for sensitivity analysis.

3. Visualize the impact of these incremental changes on your KPIs to understand which variables have the most significant impact and whether the relationship is linear, nonlinear, or complex.

Best Practices:

- Clearly define your scenarios and ensure they represent realistic and meaningful variations in your business environment.

- Use sensitivity analysis to identify the most influential factors on your KPIs. This insight can guide your focus on the most critical variables.

- Document your findings and insights from scenario planning and sensitivity analysis. This documentation can be valuable for decision-making and communication.

Scenario planning and sensitivity analysis in Tableau are powerful tools to explore different business scenarios and assess the sensitivity of your KPIs to input variables. By creating multiple scenarios and incrementally changing variables, you can gain a deeper understanding of how your business may respond to different conditions, ultimately helping you make more informed and data-driven decisions.

Creating dynamic scenarios for decision support

Dynamic scenarios in What-If Analysis are instrumental for decision support as they allow you to adapt to real-time changes and explore "what-if" questions as they occur. In this section, we'll dive into creating dynamic scenarios using Tableau for enhanced decision-making.

Step 1: Data Connection and Preparation:

1. Open Tableau and connect to your data source.

2. Ensure that you have a dataset with relevant historical data and the parameters you need for creating dynamic scenarios.

Step 2: Set Up What-If Parameters:

1. Define the parameters that will be the basis of your dynamic scenarios. For instance, if you're in the retail business, you might set up parameters for factors like demand, inventory, or pricing.

2. Create What-If Parameters in Tableau for each variable you want to control dynamically. Configure these parameters to allow user input, and specify the range or constraints for each parameter.

Step 3: Building Dynamic Scenarios:

1. Create calculated fields in Tableau that use the What-If Parameters to adjust data dynamically. For instance, if you want to create scenarios for pricing, you can build calculated fields that modify product prices based on the parameters.

2. Develop calculated fields for different dynamic scenarios. Each calculated field should represent a specific scenario, and it can be as complex or as simple as needed.

Step 4: Visualize Dynamic Scenarios:

1. Create visualizations in Tableau that incorporate the calculated fields representing your dynamic scenarios. These visualizations can be line charts, bar charts, or any relevant chart type.

2. Use your What-If Parameters as interactive controls. By setting up parameter actions, users can input values or move sliders to dynamically adjust the scenarios, and the visualizations will update accordingly.

Step 5: Decision Support and Real-Time Analysis:

1. Dynamic scenarios facilitate real-time decision support. Users can explore various scenarios, adjusting parameters as needed to assess the impact of different choices on the visualized data.

2. This real-time analysis allows you to answer questions such as "What if we increase the product price by 10%?" or "How does a 20% decrease in inventory impact sales?" in the context of your data.

Step 6: Documentation and Communication:

1. Document the dynamic scenarios and the insights gained from these scenarios. This documentation is essential for reporting, sharing insights with stakeholders, and making informed decisions.

2. Communicate your findings to relevant teams or individuals to influence decision-making processes based on the real-time insights from your dynamic scenarios.

Best Practices:

- Keep your dynamic scenarios relevant and aligned with the key variables and factors that influence your business or analysis.

- Use dynamic scenarios as a tool for collaborative decision-making, involving team members and stakeholders.

- Continuously monitor and update your dynamic scenarios as new data becomes available or as the business landscape evolves.

Creating dynamic scenarios in Tableau enables you to adapt to changing conditions, explore real-time "what-if" questions, and make data-driven decisions that are responsive to current challenges and opportunities. By incorporating dynamic scenarios into your analytics process, you can enhance your decision support capabilities and stay ahead in a rapidly changing business environment.

Goal-seeking and optimization with Tableau

Goal-seeking and optimization are powerful techniques that help you find the best possible outcome based on a specific criterion. In this section, we'll explore how to implement goal-seeking and optimization using Tableau.

Step 1: Data Connection and Preparation:

1. Open Tableau and connect to your data source.

2. Ensure that your dataset includes the relevant data for the goal-seeking and optimization analysis. This data should consist of the variables and constraints that influence the outcome you want to optimize.

Step 2: Set Up Goal-Seeking Parameters:

1. Define the goal you want to achieve and the constraints that should be considered during the optimization process. For instance, if you're in the financial sector, your goal might be to maximize profit while adhering to budget constraints.

2. Create parameters in Tableau to represent these goals and constraints. Configure the parameters to allow user input or use calculated fields to represent the constraints based on the data.

Step 3: Implementing Goal-Seeking:

1. Create calculated fields in Tableau that use the goal-seeking parameters to optimize a specific outcome. These calculated fields should represent the objective function you want to maximize or minimize.

2. Implement goal-seeking calculations in Tableau. You can use techniques such as Solver or optimization algorithms to adjust parameters and seek the desired outcome. While Tableau doesn't have built-in goal-seeking functionality, you can implement this by creating calculated fields that change based on user input.

Step 4: Visualization and Interaction:

1. Create visualizations that demonstrate the impact of goal-seeking calculations. These visualizations should show how changes in the parameters affect the optimized outcome. Common chart types include line charts, scatter plots, or data tables.

2. Use parameter controls to allow users to interact with the goal-seeking process. For example, they can adjust the budget constraint, and Tableau will dynamically recalculate and visualize the optimized result.

Step 5: Iteration and Optimization:

1. Encourage users to iterate and explore different scenarios by adjusting the goal-seeking parameters. They can experiment with various constraints and see how it affects the optimized outcome.

2. Monitor the results and guide users in finding the most optimal solution that aligns with the defined goals and constraints.

Step 6: Documentation and Reporting:

1. Document the goal-seeking process, including the objective function, constraints, and any optimizations achieved.

2. Share the insights and optimized solutions with relevant stakeholders or decision-makers.

Best Practices:

- Clearly define your goals, constraints, and the variables that impact the outcome.

- Ensure the data used in the goal-seeking analysis is accurate and up to date.

- Use visualization to make the optimization process intuitive and accessible to users.

Goal-seeking and optimization in Tableau empower you to identify the best solutions that align with your objectives while adhering to constraints. By integrating these techniques into your analysis process, you can make informed decisions and find the most optimal paths to success in various scenarios, from budgeting and resource allocation to pricing and portfolio management.

Implementing drill-down and drill-up actions

In this section, we'll delve into the implementation of drill-down and drill-up actions in Tableau. These actions allow users to interact with data hierarchies and explore detailed or aggregated information dynamically. Here's how to implement these interactive features:

Step 1: Data Preparation:

Before you can implement drill-down and drill-up actions, ensure that your dataset includes hierarchical data that you want to analyze. This data should have at least one dimension with multiple levels of granularity.

Step 2: Creating Hierarchies:

1. Open Tableau and connect to your data source.

2. Identify the dimension in your data that can be used to create a hierarchy. For example, you might have a time dimension that includes years, quarters, months, and days.

3. In Tableau, right-click the dimension you want to use for the hierarchy, and choose "Create Hierarchy." This allows you to create a multi-level hierarchy using that dimension.

Step 3: Building Visualizations:

1. Create a visualization that includes the hierarchy you've defined. This could be a bar chart, line chart, or any other relevant visualization type.

Step 4: Implementing Drill-Down Actions:

1. Right-click the visualization, and choose "Actions" from the context menu.

2. In the Actions dialog box, click "Add Action" and select "Change Hierarchy."

3. Configure the action by defining a source sheet (the sheet you're working on) and a target sheet (the sheet that will show the drilled-down data).

4. Set up the action filter by choosing the dimension that represents your hierarchy. Define how you want the action to work, such as drilling down to the next level in the hierarchy.

5. Test the action by interacting with your visualization. When you click a specific data point or dimension, Tableau should take you to a more detailed view, drilling down into the hierarchy.

Step 5: Implementing Drill-Up Actions:

1. Similar to the drill-down actions, right-click the visualization, choose "Actions," and click "Add Action."

2. Select "Change Hierarchy" as the action type.

3. Configure the action, specifying the source and target sheets.

4. Define the action filter, but this time set it to drill up to a higher level in the hierarchy.

5. Test the action by interacting with your visualization. When you click a specific data point, Tableau should take you to a less detailed view, drilling up to a higher level in the hierarchy.

Step 6: Provide User Guidance:

Consider adding instructions or a legend to your visualization to help users understand how to use the drill-down and drill-up actions effectively.

Step 7: Iteration and Refinement:

Encourage users to explore the data using these actions and gather feedback. Refine your hierarchies and actions based on user interactions and needs.

By implementing drill-down and drill-up actions, you empower users to interact with their data dynamically, enabling them to explore details or get a high-level overview as needed. This feature is especially valuable for datasets with hierarchies, such as time-based or geographical data.

Using filters for interactive data exploration

In this section, we'll explore how to use filters to enhance interactive data exploration in Tableau. Filters allow users to dynamically change the data displayed in visualizations, enabling deeper insights and customization. Here's how to implement filters for interactive data exploration:

Step 1: Data Preparation:

Ensure that your data source is loaded into Tableau and that you have created the visualizations you want to apply filters to.

Step 2: Creating Filters:

1. In the Data pane on the left, find the dimension you want to use for filtering. This could be a categorical variable, like "Region" or "Category."

2. Drag the dimension to the "Filters" shelf, which is usually located at the top of the workspace. This will create a filter for that dimension.

Step 3: Configuring Filters:

1. Once the filter is added, you'll see a control panel with various options. Here, you can select which items or values from the dimension you want to include in the filter.

2. You can choose to show all items, specific items, or only relevant values. For example, you might want to filter data by selecting specific regions or categories.

Step 4: Applying Filters:

1. To apply the filter, interact with the control panel. You can click checkboxes, use search functionality, or select values based on your preferences.

2. As you apply the filter, the visualizations on the worksheet will automatically adjust to display the filtered data. This dynamic filtering allows users to explore the data interactively.

Step 5: Leveraging Quick Filters:

Quick filters provide additional interactivity. To create a quick filter:

1. Right-click on the filter in the Filters shelf.

2. Select "Show Quick Filter."

3. A quick filter control will appear on your worksheet, enabling users to change filter settings more easily.

Step 6: Implementing Actions:

Tableau also allows you to create filter actions that connect different worksheets and dashboards. These actions enable users to click on one visualization and automatically filter another. To create a filter action:

1. Right-click on the worksheet you want to use as the source.

2. Select "Actions."

3. Click "Add Action" and choose "Filter."

4. Configure the source and target sheets or dashboards.

5. Define the filtering condition, which specifies how the selections in the source worksheet will affect the target worksheet.

Step 7: User Guidance and Exploration:

Provide instructions for users to understand how to apply filters and make the most of the interactive data exploration. Encourage them to experiment with filters to uncover insights.

Step 8: Iteration and Refinement:

Collect user feedback and analyze how they interact with filters. Refine filter options and settings to make the data exploration experience more intuitive and informative.

Using filters for interactive data exploration enhances the user's ability to drill down into specific aspects of the data, create custom views, and answer questions on the fly. It's a powerful feature that makes Tableau a valuable tool for data analysis and visualization.

Dashboard actions and URL actions

In this section, we'll dive into how to leverage dashboard actions and URL actions in Tableau to create interactive and dynamic data exploration experiences. These actions enable users to navigate through dashboards, filter data, and even connect to external resources using URLs.

Dashboard Actions:

Step 1: Create a Dashboard:

Before you can apply dashboard actions, you need to have a dashboard with multiple worksheets or components that you want to link together.

Step 2: Define a Dashboard Action:

1. Go to the Dashboard tab.

2. Click "Dashboard" in the top menu.

3. Select "Actions."

Step 3: Add a Filter or Highlight Action:

Tableau provides two main types of dashboard actions: Filter and Highlight.

- **Filter Action:** Allows you to create a selection in one worksheet that filters the data displayed in another worksheet.

- **Highlight Action:** Emphasizes selected data points in one worksheet by highlighting related data points in another worksheet.

Step 4: Configure the Action:

You'll need to configure the dashboard action settings:

1. Choose the source sheet: This is where users will interact to initiate the action.

2. Choose the target sheet: This is the sheet that will be affected by the user's interactions.

3. Define the action type (Filter or Highlight).

4. Specify the target filter field or highlight dimension.

5. Configure additional settings as needed, such as clearing the selection, hiding the source sheet, or choosing how the action should run (on hover or selection).

Step 5: Test and Save:

Click "OK" to save your action, and then test it by interacting with your dashboard.

URL Actions:

URL actions allow you to connect Tableau to external web resources, applications, or documents. This feature is useful for linking to additional information or for embedding Tableau dashboards into web pages.

Step 1: Create a Dashboard:

Similar to dashboard actions, start by creating a dashboard or opening an existing one.

Step 2: Define a URL Action:

1. Navigate to the Dashboard tab.

2. Click "Dashboard" in the top menu.

3. Select "Actions."

Step 3: Add a URL Action:

Choose "URL" as the action type. You can also specify whether the action should open the URL in a new window or use the same window.

Step 4: Configure the Action:

1. Define the source sheet or component where users will initiate the URL action.

2. Specify the URL: You can hard-code the URL or use a field in your data to generate dynamic URLs.

3. If you're using a dynamic URL, ensure that the field used is properly formatted and contains the necessary URL components.

4. Choose any additional settings, such as opening the URL in a new window or passing field values as parameters to the URL.

Step 5: Test and Save:

Click "OK" to save your action and test it by interacting with your dashboard.

User Guidance and Exploration:

Provide clear instructions for users on how to use dashboard actions and URL actions. Ensure they understand the interactive elements and external links available to them.

Iteration and Refinement:

Gather feedback from users to improve the effectiveness and intuitiveness of dashboard and URL actions. Adjust your configurations as needed to enhance the user experience.

Dashboard and URL actions significantly enhance Tableau's ability to create interactive and user-friendly data exploration experiences, making your dashboards more than just static visualizations. These actions empower users to drill down, filter, navigate, and connect to additional resources, improving data comprehension and decision-making.

Enhancing user interactivity for deeper insights

In this section, we'll explore advanced techniques to enhance user interactivity for deeper insights within Tableau. These techniques allow users to drill down into data, drill up to a higher level of aggregation, and use advanced interactions to uncover hidden patterns and insights.

Enhancing User Interactivity:

1. Drill Down and Drill Up:

  - **Drill Down:** This technique allows users to explore data at a more granular level. For example, you might have a visualization that shows total sales by year, and users can drill down to view sales by quarter, then by month, and so on.

  - **Drill Up:** On the other hand, drill up enables users to move up the hierarchy or aggregation level. Users can navigate from a detailed view (e.g., sales by month) back to a higher level (e.g., sales by quarter).

  How to Implement Drill Down and Drill Up:

  To create a drill-down or drill-up experience, you can use Tableau's hierarchy feature. Hierarchies define the relationships between dimensions, allowing users to navigate through different levels of granularity.

1. Create Hierarchies: Define hierarchies in your data model. For example, you can create a hierarchy with dimensions like Year > Quarter > Month.

2. Add Hierarchical Filters: Use these hierarchies as filters in your visualization. When a user interacts with the filter, the data automatically adjusts to show the selected level of granularity.

3. Interactive Elements: You can add interactive elements, such as buttons or parameters, to allow users to control the drill-down and drill-up experience. For example, a button labeled "Drill Down" can trigger a filter change to a more granular level.

2. Highlight Actions:

Highlight actions allow users to select data points in one visualization, which then highlights related data points in other visualizations. This technique is valuable for data exploration and analysis.

How to Implement Highlight Actions:

1. Create Highlight Actions: Configure the highlight action by defining the source and target sheets. When a user selects a data point in the source sheet, the action highlights relevant data points in the target sheet.

2. Use Parameter Controls: Add parameter controls to your dashboard to allow users to select data points interactively. Parameters can dynamically change the focus of your visualizations.

3. Interactive Filters and Parameters:

Interactive filters and parameters are powerful tools for user interactivity. Users can apply filters, set parameter values, and see real-time changes in the data visualization.

How to Implement Interactive Filters and Parameters:

1. Create Filters: You can add quick filters, range filters, and more to enable users to filter data based on various dimensions and measures.

2. Set Up Parameters: Parameters allow users to input values that affect the calculations, filters, and reference lines in your visualization.

3. Actions with Filters and Parameters: Combine filters and parameters with dashboard actions to create complex interactions. For example, a user could select a region in a filter, and the parameter value updates accordingly, affecting other visualizations.

4. Custom Calculation Groups:

Custom calculation groups are advanced features for creating user-defined hierarchies. They allow users to define their custom groups or categories in the visualization.

How to Implement Custom Calculation Groups:

1. Create Custom Groups: Define custom groups using calculated fields. These custom groups can be based on specific user-defined criteria.

2. User Interaction: Allow users to interact with these custom groups in your visualizations. For example, users might have the option to group products based on different attributes.

Best Practices:

- When implementing drill-down and drill-up experiences, ensure that the hierarchy is logical and makes sense to users.

- Combine multiple techniques for richer interactivity.

- Provide clear instructions to guide users on how to navigate and explore data.

Enhancing user interactivity in Tableau empowers users to dig deeper into their data, uncover hidden insights, and make more informed decisions. By using drill-down, drill-up, highlight actions, interactive filters, parameters, and custom calculation groups, you create a dynamic and engaging data exploration experience.

CHAPTER VI
Dashboards and Storytelling

6.1 Design principles for effective dashboards

In this chapter, we'll delve into the principles of designing effective dashboards in Tableau. Dashboards are a critical component of data visualization and storytelling, enabling you to convey insights clearly and interactively to your audience. To create impactful dashboards, you must consider various design principles and best practices.

Design Principles for Effective Dashboards:

1. Clarity and Simplicity:

- **Clear Visual Hierarchy:** Ensure that your dashboard has a clear visual hierarchy, guiding the viewer's eye through the content. Start with a title or header that sets the context and use appropriate fonts, colors, and sizes for various elements.

- **Simple Layout:** Avoid clutter and unnecessary complexity. Use a simple and organized layout that doesn't overwhelm the viewer. Place the most critical information prominently and keep non-essential elements more discreet.

2. Consistency:

- **Uniform Design Elements:** Maintain consistency in design elements such as fonts, colors, and sizing. A consistent design helps create a cohesive and professional look for your dashboard.

- **Standardized Icons and Labels:** Use standardized icons and labels to maintain consistency and make it easier for viewers to understand your dashboard.

3. Purpose and Context:

- **Define a Clear Purpose:** Know the primary purpose of your dashboard. Is it for monitoring, analysis, or storytelling? Tailor the design to align with your intended use.

- **Contextual Elements:** Provide context for the data. Include descriptions, source references, and definitions where necessary to help the viewer understand what they're seeing.

4. Data-Driven Visualizations:

- **Choose the Right Visualizations:** Select the most suitable chart types for your data and message. Ensure that the visualizations effectively convey the insights you want to share.

- **Interactive Elements:** Use interactivity wisely. Implement filters, parameters, and actions that allow users to explore data but avoid overwhelming them with too many options.

5. Performance and Responsiveness:

- **Optimize Performance:** Large datasets or complex calculations can slow down your dashboard. Optimize your queries and use data extracts to enhance performance.

- **Responsive Design:** Ensure your dashboard looks good and functions well on different devices, screen sizes, and resolutions.

6. Accessibility:

- **Design for All Users:** Create dashboards that are accessible to users with disabilities. Use alt text for images, ensure text is readable for colorblind users, and use consistent navigation for screen readers.

7. Testing and Feedback:

- **User Testing:** Gather feedback from potential users or stakeholders to refine your dashboard. Test it with a sample audience to ensure it effectively communicates your message.

- **Iterative Design:** Be ready to make adjustments based on user feedback and changing data requirements.

8. Whitespace and Flow:

- **Whitespace:** Don't be afraid of empty space. Whitespace helps separate elements and creates a cleaner and less crowded design.

- **Flow:** Consider the flow of the dashboard. Organize elements logically so that users can follow a natural path from top to bottom or left to right.

9. Engage and Tell a Story:

- **Narrative Flow:** Use your dashboard to tell a story. Start with an introduction or a compelling question and guide viewers through a narrative that leads to a conclusion or call to action.

  - **Visual Cues:** Use visual cues like annotations, callouts, or highlight actions to draw attention to important insights.

10. Branding and Personalization:

  - **Brand Guidelines:** Incorporate your organization's brand guidelines, including colors, logos, and fonts.

  - **Personalization:** Allow users to personalize certain aspects of the dashboard, such as selecting a date range or adjusting parameters.

Examples and Implementation:

- Provide specific examples and use cases where each design principle is applied effectively.

- Demonstrate how to apply these principles using Tableau, including tips on formatting, layout, and settings.

By adhering to these design principles, you can create dashboards that not only look visually appealing but also effectively communicate insights, engage your audience, and drive data-informed decision-making. Designing effective dashboards is a blend of art and science, and mastering these principles is crucial for impactful data storytelling.

6.2 Creating and customizing dashboards

Creating effective dashboards in Tableau involves combining data visualizations and interactivity to tell a compelling data-driven story. In this section, we'll explore the process of creating and customizing dashboards step by step, including examples and best practices.

Step 1: Planning Your Dashboard

Before diving into dashboard creation, it's crucial to have a plan. Consider the following:

- **Define Your Audience:** Who will be using the dashboard? What are their needs and preferences?

- **Identify Key Questions:** What questions or insights should the dashboard address?

- **Select the Right Visualizations:** Choose the most appropriate charts and graphs for your data.

- **Set Objectives:** What are the primary goals of the dashboard? Do you want to inform, analyze, or monitor?

Step 2: Building a Dashboard

Tableau makes it easy to create dashboards. Here's how:

1. Open Tableau Desktop: Start by launching Tableau Desktop.

2. Connect to Data: Connect to your data source or import a dataset.

3. Create Worksheets: Build individual worksheets to represent different aspects of your data.

4. Drag and Drop: Drag worksheets to the dashboard workspace.

5. Customize Layout: Design the layout by resizing, positioning, and organizing worksheets.

6. Add Titles and Text: Include titles, captions, and descriptions to provide context and guide the viewer.

7. Use Containers: Utilize containers (horizontal, vertical, or tiled) to organize your worksheets.

8. Create Actions: Add filter actions, highlight actions, URL actions, or dashboard actions to make your dashboard interactive.

Step 3: Dashboard Interactivity

Interactivity is a key element in engaging dashboards. Here are some interactive features to consider:

- **Filters:** Implement filters to allow users to drill down into specific data subsets.

- **Parameters:** Set up parameters for dynamic control over dimensions and measures.

- **Highlight Actions:** Use highlight actions to emphasize data points in response to user interactions.

- **URL Actions:** Link your dashboard to external web pages or documents for additional information.

Step 4: Formatting and Styling

The visual appeal of your dashboard is crucial. To format and style effectively:

- **Color Schemes:** Use a consistent color palette that aligns with your organization's branding.

- **Fonts:** Choose readable fonts and sizes for titles, headers, and labels.

- **Backgrounds:** Customize background colors or images.

- **Legends and Scales:** Format legends and scales to improve data readability.

- **Annotations:** Add annotations to highlight significant data points or trends.

Step 5: Testing and Feedback

Thoroughly test your dashboard to ensure it functions as intended. Consider different devices and resolutions, and gather feedback from potential users.

Best Practices and Tips:

- Responsive Design: Design your dashboard to be responsive across various devices and screen sizes.

- Simplify Navigation: Keep navigation and interaction options straightforward to avoid overwhelming users.

- Optimize Performance: Use data extracts and other performance optimization techniques for large datasets.

- Iteration: Be prepared to iterate on your dashboard based on user feedback and changing data needs.

Example and Implementation:

- Walk through the creation of a sample dashboard. Provide step-by-step guidance and explain the rationale behind each decision.

- Include best practices for customizing color schemes, fonts, and legends.

By following these steps and best practices, you can create impactful and user-friendly dashboards that effectively convey insights, support decision-making, and engage your audience. Customization and interactivity are key components of creating a compelling data storytelling experience.

6.3 Story points and storytelling with data

Storytelling with data is a powerful way to communicate insights, trends, and the significance of your data to an audience. Tableau provides a feature called "story points" that allows you to create a guided narrative using your visualizations. In this section, we will explore how to effectively use story points in Tableau.

Step 1: Creating a Story

1. Open Tableau Desktop: Start by launching Tableau Desktop.

2. Connect to Data: Connect to your dataset or data source.

3. Create Worksheets: Build individual worksheets or visualizations representing key points in your data story.

Step 2: Adding Story Points

Now that you have your worksheets, you can create a story using the following steps:

4. Navigate to the Story Pane: In Tableau, you'll find the "Story" pane at the bottom of the workspace.

5. Create a New Story: Click on the "New Story" button in the Story pane.

6. Add a Title: Give your story a clear and descriptive title that sets the stage for your narrative.

7. Add a Blank Story Point: Initially, you'll start with a blank story point, which is like a blank canvas for your first slide.

Step 3: Customizing Story Points

Now, you can start customizing your story points:

8. Choose a Worksheet: Select the worksheet or visualization you want to include in the first story point. Drag and drop it onto the blank story point.

9. Customize the Story Point: You can change the size, position, and layout of your visualization to suit your narrative.

10. Add Captions: Add captions, annotations, and explanations to provide context and insights about the visualization.

Step 4: Adding More Story Points

To continue your narrative, you can add more story points:

11. Duplicate Story Points: Duplicate the existing story point to create new slides in your narrative.

12. Customize Each Story Point: Modify the worksheet, layout, captions, and annotations for each story point to tell a complete story.

Step 5: Adding Navigation

Story points allow you to add navigation elements to guide your audience:

13. Add a Dashboard Navigation: Create a dashboard with navigation buttons to let users move between story points seamlessly.

14. Set Actions: Configure actions that change the story point based on user interactions.

Step 6: Preview and Refine

15. Preview Your Story: Use the "Preview" option to review your entire data story and make refinements.

16. Refine and Iterate: Be ready to refine your story and its visualizations based on user feedback and data insights.

Best Practices and Tips:

- **Simple and Clear:** Keep your story points clear and concise, focusing on key insights.

- **Engage the Audience:** Use annotations and captions to guide your audience's understanding.

- **Consistent Style:** Maintain a consistent style for all story points for a cohesive narrative.

- **Call to Action:** Encourage users to take specific actions or explore further.

Example and Implementation:

- Walk through the creation of a sample data story using Tableau, providing step-by-step guidance.

- Explain how to effectively use captions, annotations, and actions to enhance the narrative.

By following these steps and best practices, you can create compelling data stories using story points in Tableau. Storytelling with data is an excellent way to engage your audience, provide insights, and guide them through your findings.

6.4 Using actions and filtering

Interactive dashboards are a powerful way to explore and analyze data in Tableau. Actions and filtering allow you to create dynamic, responsive dashboards that provide users with a rich and personalized experience. In this section, we will explore how to use actions and filtering effectively in Tableau.

Step 1: Understanding Actions in Tableau

1. Open Tableau Desktop: Launch Tableau Desktop and open your workbook or start a new one.

2. Create Worksheets or Dashboards: Before implementing actions, you need to have worksheets and dashboards in your workbook.

Step 2: Types of Actions in Tableau

Tableau provides various types of actions, and each serves a different purpose. Here are some common types:

3. Filter Actions: These actions allow you to filter data in one visualization based on a selection in another visualization. For example, clicking on a bar chart can filter a related line chart.

4. Highlight Actions: Highlight actions emphasize the selected data points in one visualization when you select a data point in another visualization. This is useful for making connections between different views.

5. URL Actions: URL actions allow you to link to external web pages or resources based on user interactions. This can be used for drill-throughs or to provide additional context.

Step 3: Creating Filter Actions

Let's focus on filter actions for this example:

6. Select a Source Worksheet: In your dashboard, decide which worksheet or visualization will serve as the source for filtering. This is the visualization that will trigger the filter action.

7. Choose a Target Worksheet: Next, choose the target worksheet that will be filtered based on the selections in the source worksheet.

8. Create the Filter Action: Go to the "Dashboard" menu and select "Actions." Then, click "Add Action" and choose "Filter." Configure the filter action by specifying the source worksheet, target worksheet, and the fields to filter on.

9. Define the Action: Customize the filter action by specifying how the interaction should work. For instance, you can choose to clear the selection to reset the filter or apply a specific filter type.

Step 4: Implementing Highlight Actions

Highlight actions can provide additional insights:

10. Select a Source Worksheet: Choose the source worksheet that will trigger the highlight action.

11. Choose a Target Worksheet: Select the target worksheet that will be affected by the highlight action.

12. Create the Highlight Action: Follow the same steps as for the filter action but select "Highlight" as the action type. Configure the source and target worksheets, along with the fields to use for highlighting.

Step 5: Testing and Refining Actions

13. Test Your Dashboard: After configuring actions, test your dashboard to ensure they work as expected.

14. Refine and Iterate: Based on user feedback and your own analysis, refine your actions to create a seamless and informative user experience.

Best Practices and Tips:

- Clear Instructions: Provide clear instructions or tooltips to guide users on how to interact with your dashboard.

- Balanced Interactivity: Balance the level of interactivity to avoid overwhelming users.

- Use Cases: Consider different use cases and the most relevant actions for your dashboard.

Example and Implementation:

- Walk through an example of creating a filter action and a highlight action for a dashboard in Tableau.

- Explain the scenario and how these actions enhance the user's ability to explore the data.

By implementing actions and filtering in Tableau, you can create engaging and interactive dashboards that empower users to explore and gain insights from your data effectively.

CHAPTER VII
Data Sharing and Collaboration

7.1 Publishing and sharing visualizations and dashboards

In Tableau, creating insightful visualizations and dashboards is only half the journey. To make the most of your data analysis and insights, you need to share your work with others. This chapter will guide you through the process of publishing and sharing visualizations and dashboards effectively.

Step 1: Publish to Tableau Server or Tableau Online

1. Create Your Visualization: Start by creating the visualization or dashboard that you want to share. Ensure it is well-designed, informative, and visually appealing.

2. Connect to Tableau Server/Online: If you are using Tableau Desktop, you need to be connected to your Tableau Server or Tableau Online account. If you haven't already, sign in.

3. Publish Your Workbook: Once your visualization is ready, go to the "Server" menu in Tableau Desktop and select "Publish Workbook." You will be prompted to choose a project on Tableau Server/Online to publish your workbook.

4. Define Permissions: You can control who has access to your workbook. Set permissions to specify who can view, edit, or interact with your workbook. You can share it with specific users or groups, and even set it as public if it's intended for a broader audience.

5. Publish: Click the "Publish" button to upload your workbook to Tableau Server or Tableau Online.

Step 2: Sharing Options

6. Generate a Link: Once your workbook is published, you can generate a shareable link. This link can be used to share your visualization with people who have access to it. You can restrict access or make it open to anyone with the link.

7. Embed in Web Pages: If you have a website or blog, you can embed your Tableau visualization directly into a web page. This is useful for sharing data insights on your website.

8. Sharing on Social Media: Share your visualization or dashboard on social media platforms to reach a broader audience. You can either share the generated link or embed it in a post.

Step 3: Collaboration and Interactivity

9. Commenting and Annotations: Collaborators can add comments and annotations to your visualizations, enabling discussions and adding context to the data.

10. Interactivity: Tableau Server and Tableau Online allow users to interact with your dashboards. They can apply filters, drill down, and gain insights directly from the shared visualization.

11. Scheduled Updates: You can schedule your dashboards to update with the latest data at specific intervals. This ensures that your audience always has access to the most recent insights.

Best Practices and Tips:

- **Optimize for Web:** Ensure that your visualizations are optimized for web viewing. Use performance best practices to prevent slow-loading dashboards.

- **Mobile Optimization:** Check how your visualization appears on mobile devices. Ensure responsive design for better user experience.

- **Data Source Security:** Be mindful of the data sources you use. Ensure that sensitive data is not exposed through shared dashboards.

Example and Implementation:

- Walk through an example where you create a dashboard in Tableau, publish it to Tableau Server, define permissions, and share it with specific users and the public.

- Explore how your collaborators can add comments and interact with the shared dashboard to make data-driven decisions.

By mastering the art of publishing and sharing your visualizations and dashboards in Tableau, you can effectively communicate insights, collaborate with others, and drive data-informed decisions within your organization.

7.2 Permissions, security, and governance

When sharing your Tableau visualizations and dashboards, managing permissions, ensuring security, and maintaining governance are critical aspects. In this section, we will delve into these topics to ensure your data is protected, and access is controlled effectively.

Understanding Permissions:

1. Project-Level Permissions: In Tableau Server or Tableau Online, permissions are often set at the project level. Project leaders can define who has access to the entire project. This is a fundamental level of control.

2. Workbook and Dashboard Permissions: Within each project, you can further define permissions for specific workbooks and dashboards. This allows you to control who can view, edit, or interact with individual assets.

3. User and Group Permissions: Permissions can be assigned to specific users or groups. This makes it easier to manage access for teams or departments.

4. Setting Permissions: When publishing or sharing a workbook, you can specify who has permission. This can be done by Tableau administrators, project leaders, or the workbook owner.

Security Measures:

5. SSL Encryption: Ensure that SSL encryption is enabled on your Tableau Server or Tableau Online to protect data in transit. This is essential for secure sharing and viewing of visualizations.

6. Data Source Security: Control access to data sources. Define who can access, edit, or publish data sources, especially if they contain sensitive information.

7. Single Sign-On (SSO): Implement SSO for seamless and secure user authentication, making it easier to control access and maintain security.

8. Two-Factor Authentication (2FA): Encourage or require users to set up 2FA for an extra layer of security when accessing shared Tableau content.

Governance and Auditing:

9. Usage Monitoring: Regularly monitor usage of your Tableau Server or Tableau Online to ensure compliance and security. Identify who is accessing your data and dashboards.

10. Data Refresh Scheduling: Establish governance processes for data refresh schedules. Ensure that data is updated correctly without compromising security.

11. Data Policies and Standards: Define clear data policies and standards. Communicate these to your team and collaborators to ensure that data is handled appropriately.

12. Retention and Archiving: Determine data retention policies. Define how long data should be stored and establish an archiving system for older content.

Governance Best Practices:

- Governance Committee: Establish a governance committee within your organization to oversee Tableau usage, permissions, and data policies.

- Regular Auditing: Conduct regular audits to ensure that permissions and security settings align with your organization's data policies.

- Clear Documentation: Document your governance processes, so team members understand their responsibilities and data usage policies.

Example and Implementation:

- Create a scenario where you need to share sensitive financial data within your organization. Demonstrate how to set up project-level permissions, SSL encryption, and data source security.

- Explore how auditing and governance practices ensure data is protected and accessed securely by authorized users.

By ensuring the right permissions, implementing robust security measures, and following governance best practices, you can confidently share insights and collaborate with others in a secure and compliant manner using Tableau.

7.3 Alerts and subscriptions

Tableau provides a powerful feature for keeping your team updated with the latest insights—Alerts and Subscriptions. In this section, we will explore how to set up alerts and subscriptions in Tableau to ensure that your collaborators stay informed.

Understanding Alerts:

1. What Are Alerts? Alerts are notifications sent to you when certain data conditions are met. They allow you to proactively monitor your data and receive instant updates.

2. Creating Alerts: In Tableau, you can create alerts based on specific conditions, such as data thresholds, outliers, or changes in data. For example, you might set up an alert to notify you when your sales exceed a certain target.

3. Alert Delivery: Alerts can be delivered through email, web, or Tableau Mobile. You can choose the delivery method that best suits your needs.

4. Scheduling Alerts: You can schedule when alerts should run, making it easy to align with your reporting and analysis routines.

Subscriptions for Regular Updates:

5. What Are Subscriptions? Subscriptions are automated updates sent to your email inbox on a regular schedule. They provide a snapshot of your workbook or dashboard.

6. Creating Subscriptions: Subscriptions can be created for workbooks, dashboards, and views. You can specify who should receive the subscriptions and set the delivery schedule.

7. Subscription Options: You can choose from various options when creating subscriptions. For example, you can send PDF snapshots, images, or full interactive views.

Example and Implementation:

Let's consider a scenario in which you need to monitor product inventory levels. You can set up an alert to notify you when the inventory falls below a certain threshold. Additionally, you can create a daily subscription to receive a snapshot of the inventory dashboard via email. We will walk through the steps to configure these alerts and subscriptions.

Best Practices:

- **Choose Relevant Conditions:** Ensure that the conditions you set for alerts are meaningful. Too many alerts can lead to information overload.

- **Regularly Review Subscriptions:** Periodically review your subscriptions to ensure they remain relevant. Delete or update subscriptions for obsolete content.

- **Collaborate with the Team:** Work with your team to identify the right people to receive alerts and subscriptions. This ensures that the right people are kept informed.

Benefits of Alerts and Subscriptions:

- Stay informed about critical changes in your data in real-time.

- Save time by automating the process of distributing data snapshots and insights to your team.

- Empower your team to take timely actions based on the latest data.

By setting up alerts and subscriptions effectively in Tableau, you can ensure that you and your team are always up to date with the insights and data that matter most to your organization.

7.4 Collaborating with others

Collaboration is at the heart of effective data-driven decision-making. In this section, we will delve into how Tableau empowers you to collaborate with others, enabling seamless teamwork and knowledge sharing.

Tableau Server and Tableau Online:

1. What is Tableau Server and Tableau Online?

- Tableau Server and Tableau Online are platforms for sharing, collaborating, and governing your Tableau content in a secure and scalable way.

2. Publishing to Server or Online:

- You can publish your Tableau workbooks, dashboards, and data sources to Tableau Server or Tableau Online for easy access by your team members.

3. User Access and Permissions:

- Define who can access your content and what actions they can perform. You can set permissions at the project, workbook, or data source level.

Collaboration Features:

4. Commenting and Discussions:

- Users can add comments to dashboards and worksheets, facilitating discussions around data and insights.

5. Annotations:

- Add annotations directly on your visualizations to highlight specific data points or trends, providing additional context.

6. Story Points:

- Create data stories using Story Points to guide your team through a narrative built with visualizations.

7. Version History:

- View and restore previous versions of a workbook or dashboard, ensuring data integrity.

Real-time Collaboration:

8. Data Source Collaboration:

- With Tableau Prep Conductor, multiple users can collaborate on data preparation workflows.

9. Web Editing:

- Edit your dashboards in a web browser, facilitating real-time collaboration on dashboard updates.

Best Practices:

- **Effective Project Organization:** Structure your Tableau Server or Online projects logically to ensure that content is easily discoverable.

- **Consistent Data Sources:** Create and share consistent data sources to ensure that all collaborators use the same data definitions.

- **Training and Support:** Provide training and support to your team to maximize collaboration benefits.

Collaborative Benefits:

- **Faster Decision-Making:** Collaborative dashboards and insights enable teams to make informed decisions faster.

- **Knowledge Sharing:** Foster a culture of data-driven decision-making and knowledge sharing across your organization.

- **Data Governance:** Maintain control over data access and quality while allowing for collaboration.

Incorporating Tableau Server or Tableau Online into your data analysis workflow facilitates seamless collaboration and enhances your team's ability to harness the power of data for decision-making. This collaborative approach ensures that insights are accessible to those who need them, ultimately driving better business outcomes.

CHAPTER VIII
Advanced Deployment Scenarios

8.1 Deploying Tableau Server

Deploying Tableau Server is a critical step in making your Tableau content accessible to your organization. This section provides a detailed guide on deploying Tableau Server, including best practices and considerations.

System Requirements:

1. Hardware Specifications: Ensure that your server hardware meets the requirements specified by Tableau. This includes factors such as CPU, RAM, and storage capacity.

2. Operating System: Install the compatible operating system on your server machine.

Tableau Server Installation:

3. Installation Steps:

   - Tableau provides an installer that guides you through the installation process. Follow the on-screen instructions to set up Tableau Server.

4. Configuration:

- During installation, you'll be asked to configure several aspects, including data directories, gateway configuration, and authentication methods. Make sure to configure them according to your organization's needs.

Licensing:

5. License Key: Enter the license key provided by Tableau to activate your Tableau Server instance.

6. License Management:

- Learn how to manage your licenses efficiently. This may involve adding or removing licenses as your organization's needs change.

Security Considerations:

7. Firewall and Ports:

- Understand the firewall and port requirements for Tableau Server, and ensure that the necessary ports are open.

8. SSL Configuration:

- Implement SSL certificates for secure communication between Tableau Server and clients.

Server Configuration:

9. Server Settings:

- Configure server settings, such as the server name, to make your Tableau Server accessible over the network.

10. Data Sources:

- Set up data sources so that Tableau Server can connect to your data. Ensure that the necessary drivers and connections are in place.

Authentication and User Management:

11. Active Directory Integration:

- Integrate Tableau Server with your organization's Active Directory for user authentication.

12. User Roles and Permissions:

- Define user roles and permissions to control access to your content. This includes setting up user groups.

High Availability and Scalability:

13. Clustering:

- Implement clustering for high availability and load balancing.

14. Scaling Resources:

- As your organization grows, consider scaling resources such as CPU and RAM to meet the increased demand.

Backup and Recovery:

15. Backup Strategy:

- Develop a backup strategy to ensure that your data and configurations are protected.

16. Recovery Procedures:

- Have procedures in place for recovering Tableau Server in case of failures.

Monitoring and Maintenance:

17. Server Monitoring:

- Utilize Tableau's monitoring tools to keep an eye on your server's performance and usage.

18. Software Updates:

- Stay up to date with Tableau Server software updates and security patches.

Best Practices:

- Regularly update your Tableau Server instance to access new features, bug fixes, and security enhancements.

- Document your deployment processes and configurations for future reference and troubleshooting.

- Maintain a well-organized project structure to ensure that content is easy to find and manage.

Deploying Tableau Server is a crucial step in making data accessible to your organization securely and efficiently. By following the best practices and considering the various aspects outlined in this section, you can ensure a successful deployment that meets your organization's specific needs.

8.2 Embedding Tableau into applications

Embedding Tableau into applications allows you to integrate Tableau visualizations and analytics directly into your custom software applications. This chapter provides detailed steps on how to embed Tableau into your applications.

Prerequisites:

1. Tableau Server: You need a Tableau Server to publish and host your Tableau visualizations.

2. Application Development Tools: You should have access to development tools and platforms for building applications. This can be web-based, mobile, or desktop applications.

Embedding Tableau Views:

3. Publish Views to Tableau Server:

 - Create the visualizations you want to embed in Tableau Desktop and publish them to Tableau Server.

4. View URLs:

 - Retrieve the URLs of the views you want to embed. These URLs can be obtained from Tableau Server.

HTML Embed Code:

5. HTML Integration:

- To embed Tableau views, you will need to add HTML code to your application. This code can be added to a web page, mobile app, or desktop application.

6. iFrame Embedding:

- You can use an iFrame HTML tag to embed Tableau views. Specify the view's URL as the source of the iFrame.

7. Responsive Design:

- Ensure that the embedded view is responsive to different screen sizes for a seamless user experience.

Authentication and Security:

8. Authentication Methods:

- Implement authentication methods for users to access embedded Tableau views. This can include Single Sign-On (SSO) or other authentication methods.

9. Permissions:

- Set permissions to control who can access the embedded views and what actions they can perform.

Customization:

10. Toolbar Customization:

- Customize the Tableau view's toolbar to provide specific actions to your application users.

11. Filter and Parameter Actions:

- Implement filter and parameter actions to allow users to interact with the embedded view.

Error Handling:

12. Error Handling:

- Develop error handling processes to manage issues like failed view loading.

Testing:

13. Testing and Debugging:

- Thoroughly test the embedded Tableau views in your application to ensure they function as expected.

Scalability:

14. Scaling:

- Plan for scalability as your application and the number of users grow. Ensure that your Tableau Server can handle increased load.

Documentation:

15. Documentation:

- Maintain documentation for your application's users and developers, including how to interact with embedded Tableau views.

Best Practices:

- Regularly update your embedded views if there are changes to the original Tableau visualizations.

- Monitor the usage of embedded views to ensure they are performing optimally.

Embedding Tableau into applications enhances your application's data visualization capabilities, providing end-users with the power of Tableau's analytics. By following the steps and best practices in this chapter, you can seamlessly integrate Tableau into your applications, delivering valuable insights to your users.

8.3 Tableau REST API and tabcmd

Tableau provides powerful tools and APIs for advanced deployment scenarios. This chapter delves into the usage of the Tableau REST API and tabcmd for automation and programmatic interaction with Tableau Server. We will explore how to leverage these tools for various tasks.

Tableau REST API:

The Tableau REST API allows you to interact with Tableau Server programmatically. Here are some key functionalities and how to use them:

1. Authentication:

  - To use the REST API, you'll need to authenticate using your Tableau Server credentials.

2. Publishing and Managing Workbooks and Data Sources:

  - You can use the REST API to publish new workbooks and data sources to Tableau Server. This is done by making POST requests to the respective endpoints.

3. Extracts and Schedules:

  - The REST API allows you to create, refresh, and manage data extracts. You can also schedule data refreshes.

4. User and Group Management:

  - You can programmatically create, update, and delete users and groups on Tableau Server.

5. Site Management:

- Manage sites on Tableau Server, including creating new sites and configuring site settings.

6. Automation and Integration:

- Integrate Tableau with other tools and systems, such as ETL processes, to automate tasks and streamline data workflows.

7. Monitoring and Alerts:

- Use the REST API to retrieve server and site status information. You can also set up alerts based on server events.

tabcmd:

tabcmd is a command-line utility provided by Tableau for automating various tasks. It can be used for tasks such as publishing workbooks, running extracts, and more. Here's how to use tabcmd effectively:

1. Installation:

- Install tabcmd on the machine where you want to automate Tableau tasks.

2. Authentication:

- You can log in using tabcmd by providing your Tableau Server credentials.

3. Publishing Workbooks and Data Sources:

- Use tabcmd to publish workbooks and data sources to Tableau Server. You need to specify the file paths and target locations.

4. Running Extracts:

- Automate extract refreshes with tabcmd by scheduling refresh tasks.

5. Exporting Data:

- Export data from Tableau views to various file formats using tabcmd.

6. Automation Scripts:

- Create batch scripts or automation workflows that use tabcmd commands to perform complex tasks like updating permissions, deleting content, and more.

Best Practices:

- Secure your authentication tokens and credentials when using the REST API and tabcmd for automation.

- Use error handling to capture and respond to issues that may arise during automation.

- Test and validate your automation scripts in a development or staging environment before deploying to a production environment.

- Keep an eye on Tableau Server performance when scheduling automated tasks, as heavy automation can impact server resources.

The Tableau REST API and tabcmd are valuable tools for organizations looking to automate Tableau tasks, integrate with other systems, and streamline their Tableau Server management. By following the guidance in this chapter, you'll be able to harness the power of these tools effectively.

8.4 Deployment tips and best practices

This chapter provides essential deployment tips and best practices to ensure your Tableau deployment is efficient, secure, and scalable.

1. Design with Scalability in Mind:

- Plan your Tableau Server deployment with scalability in mind. As your organization grows, your Tableau deployment should be able to handle increased users, data volumes, and workloads. Ensure that the server infrastructure is designed to scale vertically or horizontally.

2. Regular Backups:

- Set up regular backups of your Tableau Server configuration, data, and content. Regular backups ensure that you can recover your data in case of hardware failure or data loss.

3. Security Best Practices:

- Implement robust security measures, including role-based access control, SSL encryption, and strong password policies. Regularly update and patch your server to protect against security vulnerabilities.

4. Content Management:

- Establish content management practices and policies to ensure that published workbooks, data sources, and dashboards are well-organized and kept up-to-date. Implement a content lifecycle strategy that includes archiving and deleting old or obsolete content.

5. Performance Optimization:

- Monitor server performance regularly and optimize workbooks and data sources for performance. Implement best practices like data source extracts, aggregation, and efficient calculations.

6. Data Governance:

- Implement data governance practices to maintain data quality, consistency, and data lineage. Define clear ownership of data sources and establish data stewardship roles.

7. Disaster Recovery Plan:

- Create a comprehensive disaster recovery plan. Ensure that backups are regularly tested, and that you have a process in place to restore Tableau Server quickly in case of a disaster.

8. Monitoring and Alerts:

- Set up server monitoring and alerts to proactively detect issues and bottlenecks. Implement monitoring tools to track usage, system resource consumption, and server health.

9. User Training:

- Provide training and resources to Tableau users so they can make the best use of the platform. Educate users on best practices for creating efficient and meaningful visualizations.

10. License Management:

- Keep track of your Tableau licenses and ensure compliance. Regularly review your license usage and consider options for optimizing licensing costs.

11. Community Engagement:

- Encourage collaboration and knowledge sharing within the Tableau user community. Foster a culture of learning and innovation.

12. Customization and Automation:

- Leverage Tableau's customization features and automation tools (e.g., Tableau REST API, tabcmd) to streamline administrative tasks and integrate Tableau with other systems.

13. Documentation:

- Maintain thorough documentation for your Tableau deployment, including installation guides, configuration settings, and best practices. This documentation is invaluable for administrators and users.

14. Regular Audits:

- Conduct regular audits of your Tableau Server deployment to ensure that it aligns with your organization's evolving needs and best practices.

15. Feedback and Improvement:

- Continuously seek feedback from Tableau users and administrators. Use feedback to make improvements to your deployment and address pain points.

By following these deployment tips and best practices, you'll be better equipped to manage and optimize your Tableau deployment, ensuring that it meets the needs of your organization and its users effectively and efficiently.

CHAPTER IX
Tips, Tricks, and Troubleshooting

9.1 Performance tuning and optimizations

Tableau is a powerful tool for data visualization and analysis, but to ensure optimal performance, it's essential to tune and optimize your Tableau workbooks and dashboards. This chapter provides you with tips and tricks to achieve peak performance.

1. Data Source Optimization:

- Start by optimizing your data sources. Use data source extracts for improved performance, especially for large datasets. Data source extracts are pre-aggregated subsets of your data, which Tableau can query more efficiently.

2. Data Filtering:

- Apply data filters judiciously. Use context filters, data source filters, and extract filters as needed to reduce the amount of data queried. Filters help Tableau focus on the relevant subset of your data.

3. Aggregation:

- Aggregating data is a powerful technique for speeding up queries. Instead of querying every data point, aggregate data where appropriate, using sum, average, or other aggregation functions.

4. Hierarchies and Drill-Downs:

   - Use hierarchies and drill-downs wisely. Implement hierarchies in your data to allow users to drill down into more granular data. This can help keep initial queries fast while providing detailed information when needed.

5. Data Source Filters:

   - Utilize data source filters to limit the data that's loaded into your Tableau workbook. By reducing the data volume, you can improve performance significantly.

6. Extract Refresh Scheduling:

   - Schedule data extract refreshes during off-peak hours. Extract refreshes can be resource-intensive, so avoid overloading the server during times of high user activity.

7. Data Source Calculations:

   - Limit the use of complex calculated fields in your data sources. These calculations can slow down query performance. If needed, use materialized calculations in the database to optimize performance.

8. Performance Recording:

   - Use Tableau's Performance Recording feature to analyze the performance of your worksheets and dashboards. Performance Recording helps identify bottlenecks and areas for improvement.

9. Dashboard Design:

   - Design your dashboards with performance in mind. Avoid adding too many complex charts or excessive detail that could impact load times. Keep your dashboards clean and focused.

10. Dashboard Size:

- Optimize your dashboard's size and layout. Smaller dashboards tend to load faster. Use device layouts to ensure the dashboard looks great on different devices without unnecessary content loading.

11. High-Performance Calculations:

- Create calculated fields that are designed for high performance. Pay attention to the level of detail and aggregation in your calculations, as complex calculations can slow down performance.

12. Usage of Parameters:

- Parameters can slow down performance if used incorrectly. Use parameters judiciously and only when necessary for user interactivity.

13. Publishing Best Practices:

- When publishing to Tableau Server, adhere to best practices for content organization and permissions. Only publish what's necessary to keep content load times down.

14. Hardware Considerations:

- Make sure the Tableau Server hardware meets your organization's needs. Proper CPU, RAM, and disk space are essential for optimal performance.

15. Continuous Monitoring:

- Regularly monitor and maintain your Tableau environment. Track performance metrics and address any performance issues proactively.

16. Training and Documentation:

- Educate your users about performance best practices. Provide documentation and training to ensure that your team is aware of optimization techniques.

By following these tips and tricks, you can fine-tune your Tableau workbooks and dashboards to deliver high-performance data visualization and analysis experiences to your users. Always remember that performance tuning is an ongoing process, and you should regularly assess and improve your Tableau deployment.

9.2 Common troubleshooting issues

Tableau is a robust platform, but like any software, issues can arise. This section addresses common Tableau troubleshooting issues and provides step-by-step guidance on how to resolve them.

1. Data Source Connection Problems:

  - **Issue:** You are unable to connect to your data source.

  - **Resolution:**

  - Verify the data source details, including the connection type, server name, port, and credentials.

    - Check if your network firewall is blocking the connection.

    - Test the connection outside of Tableau to ensure the data source is accessible.

    - Ensure that the database server is up and running.

2. Slow Performance:

  - **Issue:** Your Tableau dashboards are slow to load or refresh.

  - **Resolution:**

  - Check the performance using Tableau's Performance Recording feature to identify bottlenecks.

    - Review your data source design and query complexity.

    - Utilize data source filters, aggregation, and data extracts.

    - Optimize calculations and dashboard design for better performance.

- Ensure your Tableau Server hardware meets the system requirements.

3. Data Display Issues:

- **Issue:** Data isn't displaying as expected in your visualizations.
- **Resolution:**
  - Check your data source and verify that the data is correctly structured.
  - Examine the chart settings, including axis and mark properties.
  - Review calculated fields and measures for accuracy.
  - Inspect the use of filters to ensure they aren't hiding data.

4. Data Source Errors:

- **Issue:** You encounter data source errors, such as SQL syntax errors or data type mismatches.
- **Resolution:**
  - Carefully review your data source and SQL query.
  - Verify data types between data source and Tableau.
  - Examine calculated fields for potential errors.

5. Dashboard Publishing Errors:

- **Issue:** You can't publish a dashboard to Tableau Server.
- **Resolution:**

- Check your Tableau Server credentials and permissions.

- Ensure you have the necessary permissions to publish content.

- Review the server configuration to ensure it's accessible.

6. Data Refresh Failures:

- **Issue:** Scheduled data extract refreshes are failing.

- **Resolution:**

  - Check data source credentials and permissions.

  - Verify the data source is accessible during the scheduled refresh.

  - Examine server logs for specific error messages.

  - Adjust the refresh schedule to off-peak hours.

7. Licensing Issues:

- **Issue:** You encounter licensing problems, such as activation errors or licensing limitations.

- **Resolution:**

  - Verify that you have a valid Tableau license.

  - Check your product key or license server configuration.

  - Ensure you haven't exceeded licensing limits.

8. Tableau Server Errors:

- **Issue:** You receive Tableau Server errors, such as "server not responding" or "page not found."

  - **Resolution:**

    - Check the Tableau Server status and logs.

    - Verify network connectivity and firewall settings.

    - Ensure you have the correct URL for accessing the server.

9. Workbook Corruption:

- **Issue:** A Tableau workbook is corrupt or inaccessible.

- **Resolution:**

  - Attempt to open the workbook in a different version of Tableau.

  - Use Tableau's backup and recovery features to restore a previous version.

10. Customization Issues:

- **Issue:** You encounter problems with customizations, such as color schemes or layout design.

- **Resolution:**

  - Review your customizations for errors or conflicts.

  - Ensure you adhere to best practices for custom themes and formatting.

11. Data Security Concerns:

- **Issue:** You have data security concerns, such as unauthorized access to sensitive data.

- Resolution:

- Implement proper permissions and user access controls on Tableau Server.

- Use encryption and other security measures to protect data.

By following the steps provided for each issue, you can effectively troubleshoot common problems in Tableau and maintain a smoothly running Tableau environment. Remember that Tableau offers extensive documentation and a user community to help address specific issues not covered here.

9.3 FAQs and additional resources

In this section, we'll address some frequently asked questions (FAQs) about Tableau and provide additional resources for users who want to delve deeper into Tableau's capabilities.

Frequently Asked Questions (FAQs):

Q1. What is the difference between Tableau Desktop and Tableau Server?

- **A1:** Tableau Desktop is used for creating and editing Tableau visualizations. Tableau Server, on the other hand, is a platform for sharing, collaborating, and publishing Tableau content to a broader audience. Desktop is primarily for authoring, while Server is for sharing and managing content.

Q2. How can I speed up slow-loading dashboards?

- **A2:** Slow-loading dashboards can be optimized by improving data source design, simplifying complex calculations, and using data extracts. Additionally, use Tableau's Performance Recording feature to identify bottlenecks.

Q3. Can I automate data refreshes in Tableau Server?

- **A3:** Yes, you can schedule data extract refreshes in Tableau Server. This can be configured to run at specific intervals or times, ensuring your data is always up-to-date.

Q4. How do I create calculated fields in Tableau?

- A4: Calculated fields can be created by using Tableau's calculated field editor. You can use a formula language to define calculations. Formulas can include mathematical operations, logical conditions, and functions.

Q5. What are the best practices for designing effective dashboards?

- A5: Effective dashboard design best practices include keeping it simple, focusing on user needs, using consistent color schemes, and ensuring interactive elements are intuitive. Avoid clutter and unnecessary complexity.

Q6. How do I share my Tableau dashboards with someone who doesn't have Tableau installed?

- A6: You can share Tableau dashboards with users who don't have Tableau installed by publishing them to Tableau Server or Tableau Online. Recipients can access these dashboards via web browsers without needing Tableau Desktop.

Additional Resources:

Here are some additional resources for those looking to expand their Tableau knowledge:

1. Tableau Help and Documentation: Tableau offers comprehensive online documentation, including guides, tutorials, and reference materials. This is a great starting point for troubleshooting and learning more about Tableau's features.

2. Tableau Community: Tableau has a vibrant online community where users can ask questions, share tips and tricks, and collaborate with others. It's an excellent place to get help and exchange ideas.

3. Tableau Training and Certification: Tableau provides training and certification programs that cover various skill levels, from beginner to advanced. Completing these programs can boost your Tableau proficiency.

4. Tableau Blog: The Tableau blog is regularly updated with articles on best practices, case studies, and the latest Tableau features. It's a valuable source of information and inspiration.

5. Tableau YouTube Channel: Tableau's YouTube channel offers video tutorials, webinars, and demonstrations to help users explore Tableau's capabilities visually.

6. Tableau User Groups: Consider joining a local Tableau User Group or a virtual one to connect with fellow Tableau enthusiasts and exchange insights and knowledge.

By exploring these resources and referring to the FAQs, you can enhance your Tableau skills, troubleshoot issues, and stay up-to-date with the latest Tableau developments. Tableau's active user community and extensive support options ensure that you're never alone on your Tableau journey.

Appendix: Tableau Calculations Cheat Sheet

This appendix provides a handy cheat sheet for common Tableau calculations. These calculations are essential for creating custom fields, aggregations, and transforming data within Tableau. Below, we'll outline some frequently used calculations along with examples and explanations.

Basic Arithmetic Calculations:

- **Addition:** To create a calculated field for the sum of two fields, use the `+` operator.

    Example: `Profit + Shipping Cost`

- **Subtraction:** To find the difference between two fields, use the `-` operator.

    Example: `Sales - Returns`

- **Multiplication:** For calculating the product of two fields, use the `` operator.

    Example: `Quantity  Price`

- **Division:** To divide one field by another, use the `/` operator.

   Example: `Revenue / Units Sold`

2. Aggregation Functions:

- **Sum:** To find the total of a field, use the `SUM()` function.

   Example: `SUM(Sales)`

- **Average:** To calculate the average of a field, use the `AVG()` function.

   Example: `AVG(Temperature)`

- **Count:** To count the number of records in a field, use the `COUNT()` function.

   Example: `COUNT(Customer ID)`

3. String Manipulation:

- **Concatenation:** To combine two or more text fields, use the `+` operator.

   Example: `[First Name] + " " + [Last Name]`

- **Substring:** To extract a portion of a string, use the `LEFT()`, `RIGHT()`, or `MID()` functions.

Example: `LEFT(Product Name, 10)` (extract the first 10 characters)

- **Case Conversion:** To change the case of a string, use functions like `UPPER()`, `LOWER()`, or `PROPER()`.

Example: `UPPER(Category)`

4. Date Calculations:

- **Date Difference:** To find the difference between two dates, use the `DATEDIFF()` function.

Example: `DATEDIFF('day', Order Date, Ship Date)`

- **Date Truncation:** To extract date parts (e.g., year, month, day), use the `DATETRUNC()` function.

Example: `DATETRUNC('quarter', Order Date)`

- **Date Formatting:** To format dates as text, use the `STR()` function.

Example: `STR(Order Date, 'MMMM yyyy')`

5. Logical Functions:

- **IF Statements:** To create conditional calculations, use the `IF` statement.

Example: `IF([Sales] > 1000) THEN 'High' ELSE 'Low' END`

- **AND, OR, NOT:** To combine conditions, use `AND`, `OR`, and `NOT` operators.

Example: `IF([Category] = 'Electronics' AND [Sub-Category] = 'Tablets') THEN 'Yes' ELSE 'No' END`

6. Table Calculations:

- **Running Total:** To calculate a running total, use the `RUNNING_SUM()` function.

Example: `RUNNING_SUM(Sales)`

- **Ranking:** To rank values, use the `RANK_UNIQUE()` function.

Example: `RANK_UNIQUE(Profit)`

- **Moving Average:** To compute a moving average, use the `WINDOW_AVG()` function.

Example: `WINDOW_AVG(Sales, -2, 2)`

This cheat sheet provides a quick reference for common calculations in Tableau. As you work with more complex data and visualizations, you'll find these calculations invaluable for customizing your analyses and dashboards. Remember to adjust calculations according to your specific dataset and needs.

CONCLUSION

In this comprehensive guide, we've explored the world of Tableau from its fundamental concepts to advanced techniques. You've gained the knowledge and skills to harness the power of Tableau for data visualization, analysis, and storytelling. From the basics of connecting to data sources, to crafting interactive dashboards, and sharing insights with your team, this book has equipped you with the tools to make data-driven decisions.

The journey through Tableau has taken you through various chapters, each building upon the previous one. You've learned how to transform raw data into meaningful insights, perform statistical analyses, create compelling visualizations, and leverage the full potential of Tableau's features. You've explored data blending, scenario planning, dashboard design, and advanced deployment scenarios.

But the learning doesn't end here. Data and analytics are dynamic fields, and Tableau is continually evolving. We encourage you to stay curious, explore new features, and push the boundaries of what's possible. As you continue your Tableau journey, remember that practice and exploration are your best allies. Experiment with real-world data, engage with the Tableau community, and learn from your experiences.

We'd like to extend our sincere appreciation for choosing this book as your guide. We hope it has been a valuable resource on your path to becoming a Tableau expert. Your commitment to learning and improving your data visualization skills is commendable, and we're confident that you'll find Tableau a powerful tool for your professional journey.

Thank You:

We'd like to express our gratitude to each and every reader who has invested time, effort, and trust in this book. Writing this comprehensive guide has been a labor of love, and it's our hope that it has been a helpful resource on your Tableau journey. We're immensely thankful for your support.

We would also like to thank the Tableau community, whose vibrant and collaborative spirit continues to inspire us. Your passion for data and visualization is contagious, and it drives us to create resources like this book.

As you embark on your Tableau adventures, we wish you success in your data visualization endeavors. May your analyses be insightful, your dashboards engaging, and your storytelling compelling. We hope you continue to find joy in exploring data and uncovering hidden insights.

Thank you for being a part of our Tableau community. Here's to a data-filled future filled with meaningful discoveries and impactful insights.

Sincerely,